SAMANTHA DEE

My Big Fat Fat

What I've learned from a lifetime of dieting

First published by Dream Eclectic Publishing 2021

Copyright © 2021 by Samantha Dee

All rights reserved. No part of this publication may be reproduced, stored or transmitted in any form or by any means, electronic, mechanical, photocopying, recording, scanning, or otherwise without written permission from the publisher. It is illegal to copy this book, post it to a website, or distribute it by any other means without permission.

Samantha Dee asserts the moral right to be identified as the author of this work.

Samantha Dee has no responsibility for the persistence or accuracy of URLs for external or third-party Internet Websites referred to in this publication and does not guarantee that any content on such Websites is, or will remain, accurate or appropriate.

Second edition

ISBN: 9798737284800

This book was professionally typeset on Reedsy.
Find out more at reedsy.com

Dedicated to my Dad, who is the best human being on this planet. And all my family and friends who encouraged me to put this to paper.

Contents

Foreword	v
A is for	1
Aches and Pains	2
Acid Reflux	5
Anxiety	7
B is for	8
Base Metabolic Rate	9
Bath Time	11
Beauticians	14
Blood Sugar Diet (Review)	17
Bras	23
C is for	31
Cafés	32
Calories	34
Cambridge Diet (Review)	36
Catfishing	37
Change	38
Change One Thing	40
Cheating	41
Clothing Sizes	43
Count	44
D is for	45
Dating	46
Diet	47
Diet Pills	49
Doctors	51

E is for	53
Exercise	54
F is for	57
Falling off the Wagon	58
Fatigue	60
Fat Lumps	62
Fat-Shaming	63
Fear	71
Femininity	72
Fluids	74
G is for	75
Gastric Band	76
Gimmicks	82
H is for	83
Habits	84
Hunger	85
Hunger-Scale	87
I is for	89
Incontinence	90
J is for	92
Jargon	93
Jaw Winking Syndrome	94
Jersey	95
K is for	97
Kidnapping	98
Kindness	99
L is for	101
Lists	102
Lighter Life (Review)	103
M is for	107
Massage	108
Metabolism	109
Men	110

Mindfulness	112
Mood Swings	113
Mirrors	114
N is for	116
Necessity	117
Needles	118
Negativity	119
Noting	120
Nutrition	121
O IS FOR	122
Obesity	123
P is for	124
Panic Attacks	125
Plateaus	126
Preparation	128
Q is for	133
Quick Fixes	134
R is for	135
Realism	136
Reasons (and Excuses)	137
Rosacea	138
Rubbing	140
S is for	141
Self Esteem	142
Sizes	144
Skirts	145
Slimfast 1-2-3 Plan (Review)	146
Snoring	149
Socks	150
Spas (Health/Beauty Spas)	153
The Special-K Plan (Review)	154
Summer	157
T is for	158

Tables	159
Talcum Powder	160
Temperature	161
Time	163
Toning Tables	164
Train Seats	165
Triggers	166
U is for	167
Uniform	168
V is for	170
Visualization	171
W is for	173
Waxing	174
Weightwatchers (Diet Review)	175
Why	178
X is for	180
X-Rated (Love, Sex, and Dating)	181
Y is for	192
Yoga	193
Z is for	194
Zee End of the Book	195
Bibliography	197
Epigraph	199
More by Samantha	201
An Excerpt from 'The Sequel'	202
About the Author	203
Also by Samantha Dee	205

Foreword

I love it when it snows. Since I've been in my new house, I've wanted at least a foot of snow to fall, so that I can go out into my new garden, plop down, and make a 'snow angel.'

Unfortunately, when you refrain from doing this -for fear of throwing up a snow cloud the size of a small county -you know you've got a problem, other than the weather.

I've been overweight (and dieting) all my life, and just lately I've become acutely aware of what we don't talk about at those weigh-in classes - the other things we might suffer as a result. Yes, we are all beautiful; but hey, being overweight is not how we were built when we floated out of the maelstrom.

I am not a doctor or a dietician, and I have absolutely no medical qualifications whatsoever. I have, however, been on just about every diet that exists on the planet and I'd like to share my experiences with you.

I hope you find something you identify with in this book, or at least can laugh at, or maybe even something that makes you think, Gosh, I thought it was just me! My story is completely honest, and a bit silly. If you can perhaps say, 'I know, right!' then I'll be forever accomplished.

Much love to you.

MAITRE D: And finally, monsieur, a wafer-thin mint.
  MR. CREOSOTE: Nah.
  MAITRE D: Oh, sir, it's only a tiny, little, thin one.
  MR. CREOSOTE: No. Fuck off. I'm full.
> –Monty Python, The Meaning of Life

A is for

Aches and Pains

My, we started off with a happy subject, didn't we? Sorry about that, it gets funnier, honest.

Love, Debbie Downer.

I can't tell you how many times I've had days off work here and there because of aches and pains. Largely due to the fact that I'm voluntarily carrying an extra person on my back.

Honestly, if I were murdered right now, my chalk outline would be a circle.

Once a while back, while walking to my car, headed to work, my right foot just sort of exploded into a painful spasm, for no apparent reason whatsoever. Luckily, there was no one around to see me double-over like Quasimodo.

It's a dangerous path to reach for the painkillers every time that happens.

Over the years I've found the most inexpensive and helpful solution when dealing with pain is walking. Just walking. Gently, carefully, and regularly.

I find walking helps me the most, particularly with back pain. You see, what happens with back pain is that I am very likely to flinch away it, so then my muscles 'spasm' to protect the original source of pain. Eventually, this will continue to happen until the spasm itself hurts, on top of the original pain.

In September 2012, I prolapsed one of my discs while stepping down a step that was higher than I thought it was. I felt it go, and within hours I was navigating the staircase on my butt and using a computer chair to wheel myself around the house.

I called the Emergency Doctor out, managing to unlock my front door and open a window near the door, so he/she could hear me shout, 'Come in!' and I wouldn't have to get up.

I was on the couch when she showed up. She knocked on the door. I shouted, 'Come in – I can't move!'

Again, she knocked on the door.

I shouted, 'Come in. I can't move!'

In the end, she un-knowingly forced me to crawl to the door and let her in.

'Well,' she said, walking behind me as I shuffled back to my couch, holding onto the furniture for stability, 'What seems to be the problem?'

Of course, it's not obvious at all, I thought to myself as I rolled onto the couch in agonizing slow-motion. After I had explained to her what the problem was, she had me lie on my back.

Time slowed when I saw her reach out, grab for my left ankle, and begin lifting it up off the couch toward the ceiling.

'Does this hurt?' she asked.

I almost screamed, inhaling a very sharp and loud 'hiss' before almost biting my lip in two. She was startled, and literally dropped my ankle.

Then I actually screamed.

'Yes, I definitely think you've got a disc problem.'

No shit, Sherlock.

I didn't say anything. Mostly because I was speechless from pain after she dropped my leg.

'Do you have any painkillers in the house?'

I told her no and begged her to prescribe unconsciousness. So, she did. I was prescribed with paracetamol, codeine, anti-inflammatories, Tramadol, and Diazepam.

Before she left, she turned to my immobile body on the couch and said,

'And be careful with lifting and carrying.'

She had gone before I could respond.

After a couple of days of being immobile and knocked out, I was numb enough to stand up and take some steps, without holding onto furniture or bursting into tears and blowing snot-bubbles.

After that, I would go outside and walk around my backyard. And so on. Recovery felt most efficient when I was walking upright – naturally and slowly. This gently untangled the muscles that had been protecting my disc from further aggravation.

Once walking was bearable, I made a few appointments with the Chiropractor.

I was back to work after a month.

I've learned that gentle exercise and six-monthly visits to a chiropractor for a tune-up, has kept me pain free and, more importantly, pain-killer free ever since.

While I am overweight, I have to continue to look after my joints and muscles. That episode is not one I'd care to repeat.

Acid Reflux

I was eating so badly for such a long time that my body began to really hate me. One of the ways that hatred manifested was through acid reflux.

It's literally pure stomach acid, bubbling up in such an angry way that it works its way up into my mouth. It's basically my body trying to kill me while I sleep.

I'll wake up with a choking reflex, and this absolutely foul acid in my mouth. It's vile, scary -painful because it burns my esophagus -and it takes hours for the hideous taste to go away. Although cookie-dough ice-cream helps.

It tends to flare up if I eat anything even remotely spicy. I think the worst episode I had was when I was driving to work the morning after I'd eaten some spicy food.

There I was, eighty-miles-an-hour on the motorway in commuter traffic, singing out loud, when, 'whoosh!' stomach acid.

It scared me half to death because it usually just happens when you are horizontal. Plus, I was driving at the time. Perhaps it was the Bon Jovi on the radio.

I pulled into the nearest service station and bought half a litre of that pink gunk you can drink to settle your stomach. You know, the stuff that tastes like liquorice cement.

When I arrived at work I sat calmly and ate two bananas, (bulky enough to drag the taste of acid back down, and there's nothing in bananas that's likely to aggravate my insides).

How lady-like; I feel I've reached the very epitome of femininity.

It has been over three years since I've eaten anything spicy (not something you forget twice, I should add), and I know that my self-treatment works, in case it happens again.

In the long term, if this keeps happening, I will see a Doctor. That stomach acid isn't supposed to 'be' anywhere else other than the stomach, and I envision it doing some great damage elsewhere.

Oh, and if I'm feeling 'pukey' I find it best to eat something I don't mind bringing back up again.

Sounds gross, but hey, if you've ever hurled up a tandoori-chicken, you'll know what I'm talking about.

Anxiety

Being overweight has in the past deeply affected my self-esteem and sense of worth, and I believe this eventually developed into a more permanent anxiety disorder. It was, at least, one of the contributing factors.

I had therapy every week for a year back in 2010, and I learned some startling things about myself, some of them life-changing: I'm 'petulant' around food and I have a tendency for 'secret eating' because of things that happened to me in my past. After that period of treatment, things were much improved for several years. I'd definitely learned more about myself and my self-esteem had recovered considerably.

Then in 2016, out of nowhere, I had several frequent anxiety attacks which were completely random, (one whilst standing in a queue for coffee, once on a train, once at work while I was in a meeting).

After some of my own research and a Doctor's visit, the anxiety attacks were attributed to the chemical changes that happen during menopause, so I don't think it's related to being overweight.

However, I don't think it's unreasonable to suggest that anxiety and being overweight might have something in common.

The best reference material regarding Anxiety is from your Doctor (and not all the crap on the internet).

See also Self Esteem.

B is for

Base Metabolic Rate

Here's what I learned about how many calories I need in a day. The formula gets a bit heavy (see what I did there?) but it's worth knowing. BMR is the number of calories I burn, at rest. There is a basic formula I use to calculate it after a bit of research. Here it is. Fear not and stay with me here, I will explain. This is called 'The Mifflin St Jeor Equation, 1990':

$$P = \left(\frac{10.0m}{1\,kg} + \frac{6.25h}{1\,cm} - \frac{5.0a}{1\,year} + s \right) \frac{kcal}{day}$$

The Mifflin St Jeor Equation, 1990

And this is what it means:
- P = Heat produced (calories burned) at rest (BMR) equals:
- m = Mass (your weight, in KG) x 10 +
- h = Height (in CM) x 6. 25 −
- a = Age (in YEARS) x 5
- s = +5 for males and −161 for females

Then, multiply by your activity level ('exercise' below means increasing heart rate for at least 30 minutes):
- Sedentary (desk job, don't really exercise): x 1. 2

Light Activity (exercise 1-3 times a week): x 1. 375
Moderate (exercise 3-5 times a week): x 1. 55
So, mine would be: m657.7 + h950 −a250 − s161 x 1.2: **1436.04**

* * *

This is pivotal for me to understand in my mind: the actual science of losing weight. To explain further, this is how I've interpreted it (and why I do NOT believe the diet books when they quote one single daily calorie requirement for women and one for men):

Everyone has a different BMR. Imagine a normal weight twenty-year-old, and an overweight fifty-year-old. Biologically, I reckon it would take a lot more work for the body to keep the overweight fifty-year-old alive and breathing.

Remember that calories, which all my life have been conditioned to think and believe are hell spawn, are fuel for things. Sneezing, stretching, shagging, sleeping, pooping, all burns calories; my BMR is what all this is for – and so, in all likelihood, this will change in a small way every day. I might be under stress, fighting an infection, or having a lot of sex (please?).

So, what do I do with this information? To maintain my current weight, eating up to my BMR will mean my weight will stay the same. It helps to get comfortable with the amount of calories I actually need before I decide to lower that in order to lose weight.

Half the battle is knowing that eating the slice of black velvet cake in the Godiva Chocolate Café in Harrods, will put me over what I need. And that this gorgeous cake will likely turn into several billion stored fat cells.

This section might have been frown-worthy to read. I'm right with you; but hey, it's science. Doodling was always more my thing.

See also Calories

Bath Time

There are three types of bath/shower time for me. One is the 'hop in, wash on, wash off' workday bath time.

Second, is the 'going out -use every product I own' bath time, and the final one is the 'light candles and lay like a raisin' bath time.

I'm not really one for bath time number three, since the moment I've lit all the candles and climbed in, I start thinking about what else I could be doing. I also normally have some kind of (fat-related) ache or pain or some such, which tends to make the whole experience not that comfortable anyway.

Number Two would be my favorite, although I find that, being on the larger side, bath time is just not like it is in the movies: the lady in the famous razor ads, under a waterfall, floating a leg up in the air as if she's climaxing whilst gracefully gliding a razor down her oiled, forty-two-inch legs. It's just not happening with my little tree stumps.

Even less realistic are TV ads where a twelve-year-old with radiant, 'baby-skin' is lathering her face to clean those 'black heads' (that she doesn't have), before splashing her face with abandon, as if she isn't then going to turn around and slip in the water, she's unwittingly splashed all over the bathroom tile and break her neck.

By the time I've razor'd, loofa'd, waxed, plucked, polished, masked, and pumiced myself to within an inch of my life, I'm exhausted, aching, and have lost all enthusiasm for going out in the first place.

In my experience, when I've been severely overweight, all this luxurious pampering is quite an effort -stretching this way and that, holding hair dryers, even polishing toenails can contort me into such impossible positions that it all becomes an ordeal. By the end of it, I'm sweating like a hog, my makeup has melted off, and the hot straightening irons have made my scalp sweat, causing my hair to frizz.

My solution was to opt for number one: do as little as possible, as quickly as possible, with the highest quality products I can possibly afford.

I try and make the shower/post-shower fragrance match (ooh, hark at me, Estee Lauder would be jealous), and I have a day fragrance and a night one (again, I say 'hark'). I'm not saying that because I'm a snob, but because wearing the right fragrance can make me feel clean, fresh, and classy during the day, and vamp super-girl at night.

When you are fat, anything that can make you feel more comfortable equals a little bit more confidence in my book (well, this book actually). This in turn gives me one less thing to think about, and more 'mind-space' to either apply myself during the day or enjoy myself at night.

I've learned that hair and nails are things which do change when overweight, depending on my diet, so it's worth spending a bit extra to have as immaculate a turnout as I am able. If I smell classy with beautiful hair and nails, I'll feel it. Fat (and elasticated trousers) be damned.

I'm lucky enough to be able to afford to get my hair done every two weeks, be it cut, color, or just a blow dry. I also get gel overlays on my nails every two weeks.

I also invest in a really good 'nude' nail varnish; Revlon's no. 900 'Pink Nude' is absolutely beautiful, no matter how many coats I apply, or how dastardly I am at applying it. Additionally (or instead), any of the Opi 'Nail Envy' range will keep my nails looking tippy-top.

For day-fragrance, I'm really not into wearing 'full-on' perfume. I had an episode in a train carriage once, where the lady sitting next to me decided to spray hers, and I was choking for air for the rest of the two-hour journey. I find most of them a teeny bit obnoxious (I must be showing my age).

I try and find shower/bath gel and body crème to match. I use Clarins treatment fragrances – 'Eau Ressourçante' in spring/summer and 'Eau Dynamisante' in winter. They make me feel like a million bucks. I know, that makes me sound like such a tart. I can't really explain them, they are not perfumes per say; they are body sprays.

Hair-wise, I get my hair cut every six weeks at a good salon. A bit of pampering is empowering, is it not? I really can't face a full-on beauty routine, so I choose a few quick, classy products—whatever makes me feel good, and get on with my life.

Beauticians

Beauticians are just about the only strangers who will see me in a state of undress, and who will put their hands 'on' me. They keep their tone of voice light and pleasant and pretend not to notice when I accidentally 'toot' as I get up off the treatment table.

My earliest memories of these experiences go back to the eighties – to a health spa that my mother and I joined, called 'The Roman Way.' We'd visit after we'd gone to Slimming World (my mum was a Slimming World 'leader' for a spell) and we'd swim, sauna, jacuzzi, and have a session on the sunbeds.

Sometimes we'd go before the weigh-in and have an hour in the sauna to lose half a pound before turning up.

There weren't really beauticians at this place. However, it made us feel healthier and pampered, even if we did have a tuna-mayo baguette in the bar before we left. Health spas, even this tiny one, were 'all the rage' in the eighties, you know.

As far as Beauty Salons go, they were the epitome of luxury and indulgence to me. They still are. When I was a healthier weight, I'd have all kinds of treatments.

The first salon I went to, was a 'Clarins' salon, and one of my fondest memories was a day visit that I booked in preparation for a Christmas party. (During said party, I danced on tables, and so can't have been that fat; none of them collapsed). Anyway, I'd booked an entire day, with just about every treatment I could possibly have at once.

There I was, on the treatment table, wearing paper knickers, wrapped up in cling film, mud, and some electric pulse thing, with one lady doing a facial, one doing my nails, and the other doing a pedicure. I felt utterly pampered. I lost half an inch off my waist, apparently. Yes, I was hooked.

As the weight went on, I grew less and less confident with the paper knickers and cling film, and so stuck to facials, pedicures, and nails. (That way I don't have to undress or show any fat bits, and they don't have to touch them).

One time, I thought I'd push the boat out and went to get my legs waxed. I walked into the treatment room and there was the little pot of wax in the heater on the side-table. The little muslin strips and little wooden applicators laying neatly next to it. She took one look at my legs and I could almost hear her saying to herself,

'We're gonna need a bigger boat.'

Subsequently, she brought out an industrial-sized waxing machine that applied the hot wax in great swathes and table-cloth lengths of muslin to rip it off.

'Okay,' I thought, *'I'll just shave in the bath.'*

Eventually, even facials turned out to be traumatic; I hated lying flat because of back pain, and they always want your 'shirt-off.' One quite horrifying facial took place at a renowned health spa (anywhere that has heated waterbeds is nirvana in my book); the beautician clearly took ill to me. (I know that sounds paranoid, but I've been in the service industry), and her shoulder-neck massage turned into an agonizing ordeal. I think she thought that, as I was overweight, she had to squeeze harder to get to my muscles. That day I went home bruised across my shoulders and I was a little too embarrassed and traumatized to say anything.

I visited another spa with a friend as a treat, as we'd both lost thirty pounds each that year, and so I thought I'd push the boat out. I plucked up the courage to get a body scrub. Different beautician, same bruises, only this time on my legs. Since then, I've stuck to manicures.

Only very recently, (and after more significant weight loss) have I had the courage to get a pedicure with the same lady who has done my nails.

She was excellent; although, she had to convince me that she has seen worse. She told me that she practiced her pre-qualification skills in her home village in Hungary -on an old man who had never worn shoes his entire life,

like the werewolf-feet in those old movies.
Thanks, love.

Blood Sugar Diet (Review)

I decided to try this recently, on account of how poorly I felt at the time. Just about every symptom of being fat was flaring up and I felt like a miserable sack of wet sand. What I liked about this diet was that the food and recipes sounded clean and pleasant. So, I bought the book on Kindle.

Using my preparation (*see Preparation*) I studied the recipes and decided which one appealed to me. As I've mentioned elsewhere in this book, this particular diet mapped out my meals for eight weeks. For the first week, I chose meals that I could easily prepare -nothing too complicated. I chose about three from each meal group:

Breakfasts:

- No carb bircher: 180 calories -Serves 1
- Blueberry and Green Tea shake: 100 calories -Serves 1
- Spinach & Raspberry green "drink": 70 calories -Serves 1

Lunches:

- Courgette and feta salad: 270 calories -Serves 1
- Beetroot Falafels: 290 calories -Serves 2
- Grapefruit and Manchego salad: 280 calories -Serves 2

Fridge-Pickers:

- Beetroot hummus: 200 calories
- Minted pea hummus: 170 calories

Suppers:

- Lamb & Pine-nut meatballs with Moroccan
- salad Crab cakes: 440 calories - Serves 1
- Foil Steamed Fish: 370 calories - Serves 2
- Spicy turkey & apricot burgers with salad: 460 calories - Serves 2

Brunches:

- Edam & Pecans: 320 calories
- Tuna and spring onion
- No Carb Ploughman's: 290 calories

Simple Suppers:

- Lime & Ginger Chicken Breast: 130 calories (+chicken)

* * *

My grocery list for one week was enormous:

- *flour (smallest cheapest possible)*
- *sliced ham*
- *50ml apple juice*
- *cheddar cheese (smallest possible)*
- *200 ml coconut water*
- *edam (smallest possible)*
- *2 x eggs*
- *40 g feta cheese*

BLOOD SUGAR DIET (REVIEW)

- *Greek yoghurt (large pot)*
- *Manchego cheese (smallest possible)*
- *plain yoghurt (small pot)*
- *1 x apple*
- *2 x avocado*
- *1 x bag baby spinach (smallest possible)*
- *1 x beef tomato*
- *50 g blueberries*
- *1x head broccoli*
- *1xcarrot*
- *1xbunch celery*
- *50 g cherry tomatoes*
- *fresh coriander*
- *1 x courgette*
- *cucumber 1/2*
- *fennel bulb*
- *fresh flat leaf parsley*
- *fresh parsley (curled/whatever)*
- *1 bag fresh mint*
- *1xbulb garlic*
- *50 g green beans*
- *1 large pink grapefruit (or red/whatever)*
- *5x lemons*
- *3xlimes*
- *5xmushrooms*
- *1xonion*
- *pot pomegranate seeds*
- *1x tub raspberries*
- *raw beetroot (whatever you can get)*
- *bag red chili (or 1, if loose)*
- *1xred onion*
- *2x bags rocket leaves*
- *1x bag spinach leaves*

- 7x spring onions (1x bunch?)
- 1xpack salad tomatoes (or 1, if loose)
- pack fresh chicken breast (or frozen, whatever)
- pack fish fillet (or 1x fillet)
- pack minced lamb (as close to 100g)
- 200 g peas (fresh/garden, can or frozen)
- 1xpack turkey mince
- 2x can chickpeas
- 1x can crabmeat
- 1x sweetcorn
- jar tahini paste
- 1x small can tuna
- 1x bag whole almonds blanched
- jar whole cumin seeds
- 1x bag dried apricots
- 1x bag ground flaxseed (expensive!)
- 1x bag pecan nuts
- 1x bag pine-nuts
- 1x pack snack box raisins
- 1x small pack flaked almonds
- 1x small bag walnut pieces
- 1x small bag walnut halves
- 1x cheapest bottle balsamic
- 1xjar chutney (low sugar if poss.)
- 1x tiny jar mayonnaise
- 1x cheapest bottle olive oil
- 1x bottle dark soy sauce
- 1x bottle Thai fish sauce (or, if that makes stomach turn, I'd try soy)
- 1x bottle vegetable oil (smallest possible)
- 1x bottle Worcestershire sauce
- 0.5 tsp 5-spice (or whatever similar)
- 0.5 tsp Baharat spice (if you can find it, or ground mixed spice)
- Green tea bags (not flavored, tried that in recipe, yuck)

- *jar cayenne pepper*
- *jar ground cumin*
- *jar ground all spice*
- *jar ground cinnamon*
- *jar paprika*
- *salt & pepper (black pepper, not that nasty table stuff)*
- *water*

Total spent: **£83.71** (to serve 1, for a week), And that's choosing the cheapest/smallest possible items. Can you believe that?

* * *

Granted, this list is assuming I have nothing at all, so there's a good chance I have a lot of the spices and oils in the back of my 'cupboard of doom'. Plus, a lot of the ingredients purchased are good for more than one meal (like the flour, or the drink that needs one teabag -you know, they don't sell those in singles).

I tell you, when this stuff arrived on my doorstep I about fainted. I barely had room for it all in my tiny kitchen. (In fact, I didn't). And I was affronted with things I'd never even seen before. Anyone buy raw beetroots regularly?

After that initial shock and having packed (more like stuffed) everything away, I thought I'd prepare myself an evening meal and see how that went.

While preparing the meal, I was inserting the ingredients into my 'MyFitnessPal' app and found that a lot of the calories stated for the meals were different than what's stated in the book, some very different in fact.

The recipe descriptions aren't all that consistent either. They jump from, 'one lemon, juiced' to 'some lemon juice.' 'flat leaf parsley' to 'some parsley.' 'baby spinach leaves' to 'spinach' (can't imagine there's that much of a difference). The recipes also switch from 'Serves 1' to 'Serves 2' which requires a good amount of attention.

Finally, and possibly most importantly, variation in phrases like: 'a small piece of' and 'a dollop' when talking about cheese and mayonnaise, this is just dangerous.

Mate, you wanna see the size of my dollops?

That said, I really liked this meal plan. I can see myself eating this way permanently. Which is the key really, isn't it? I have to find the type of food I like, practice preparing it, and keep doing it. There's no point in choosing a meal plan that features a lot of spicy food if I can't tolerate spices.

The book itself goes into an intense amount of details regarding diabetes, which is interesting to know. Personally, I think everyone should be educated on this subject, especially if they are displaying symptoms. I will try and carry on with this one.

Bras

'She wore no brassiere underneath, and he regarded her breasts somberly.'
  – Ten from Infinity, Paul W Fairman.

I could almost guarantee that every female I know owns at least four bras, which vary in size. I recently posted a survey on Facebook to my female friends, and the results showed that eighteen women owned a total of two hundred and fifty bras. That's a flat average of thirty-one bras each. Of those bras, each gal declared having at least two varied sizes, some more than four.

Yea Gods, shouldn't it be a law that every bra fits the same when you put it on, regardless of cup style? On top of the manufactured size, they all have their foibles, poking or chafing in diverse ways, not sitting right, not shaping in the same way.

The available choice tends to lessen the bigger I get; although these days, I have to say that things have improved many-fold.

Here's what I consider to be an ideal bra:

- A bra should make our boobs look feminine and perhaps glamorous, not like tired, flat sausages aiming at the floor.
- The larger the bra size, the wider, longer, and more adjustable the shoulder straps should be. You try carrying two gala-melons with two shoelaces.
- The length of the bra band should be as per the label, when stretched.

- Armpit lumps should not spill over the band.
- The wires should not be made from recycled razorblades.
- The wire should not stop an inch away from the end of its casing (like the one I'm wearing currently).
- The central piece at the front shouldn't make us feel like we've donned Joan of Arcs armour.
- The fabric encapsulating the wire is such that the wire can't "peek" through and stab holes in our armpits.
- The wire is either flexible or strong enough not to snap in two, making one boob look like a deflated dinghy halfway through your day.
- The bra doesn't give us boob-sweat.
- I don't want to have to adjust anything, at any time of the day, ever.
- I don't want to feel the darn thing!

* * *

Now, let me raid my underwear drawer and describe each bra, why I bought it and why I subsequently don't wear it. These being the best, funniest and strangest ones:

38D Hot Pink

A corset style bra with vertical bones in the cup, which makes it look like I'm wearing a corset on each boob. I don't wear it because the middle vertical bone in each cup doesn't shape 'around' my boob; it just sticks straight up. So, if I bend down to pick something up off the floor, I stab myself in the chin.

36B Red

Probably my second favorite bra of all time... I've cut the ticket out of this so I'm guessing 36B. This was a Christmas present in the eighties from my mum and was part of a set. Our dog at the time ate the knickers. It's a vintage true red, all lace, and makes my boobs look super-glam, á la pin-up. (I'll get back into it one day).

The reason I don't wear this is because it's my favorite bra, and I'm scared to break it.

42E Black

Looks like a traditional, over-the-shoulder-boulder-holder. You know, the Playtex 'Doreen' vibe. The reason I don't wear this is because it's NOT underwired, and I've yet to find a wireless bra that is remotely supportive and doesn't make your boobs look like sagging dog ears. There are huge, thick, padded straps on this. Honestly, it's a monstrosity. Also, I've never been an E-cup, so not sure what I was thinking? comfort and invisibility, probably?

38D Black

This one is from Victoria's Secret "Body by Victoria" range. I used to wear these all the time -absolutely loved them. They are really comfortable: they've got formed cups, and beautiful, stretchy soft fabric. The wires are nicely enclosed. The only reason I don't wear this one is because it's too small now, and the wires dig in, making me miserable. I think I had to stop buying them because VS started messing with the design and changed the fabric. Why do they do that? If it ain't broke, don't fix it.

38D Pale Pink

This is a lovely, dusky, vintage pale-pink color with lace overlay and half-pads. Half shoelace straps. It's a very pretty bra, fairly comfy. I wore this quite a lot. Creates monster-cleavage. Gone up four sizes or so now, so I'll keep it just in case they deflate.

42D Wine

This one is possibly from a multi-pack. It has nice thick straps, and it's underwired, not padded. Polka-dot lace. When I hold this up in front of me, it looks very 'compact', so I suspect that I don't wear this one because it smashes my boobs together, like a large version of two tomatoes stuffed unsuccessfully into an egg cup. Bought it because of the beautiful color.

42C Coral

Bought this one this year, actually. In 2016-17 I've floated between 42C and 44C. It's underwired, not padded, and sheer. I wanted a 'summer' bra with very little fabric and very little 'hardware' in the front-centre. I was so excited when I ordered this. However, I was utterly disappointed with this when I tried it on. The wires are super flimsy, and there's no support in this bra whatsoever. My boobs looked like two gala melons in a sausage skin. I might as well wear a bikini top. It's a real shame actually -could have been a perfect summer bra. Manufacturers should really test their larger sizes. This might have been my all-time favorite.

38C Black Body Suit

Oh! Forgot I had this. There's no size on it, (I went through a phase of cutting the tickets out of everything). It's black with underwired cups and cream lace trim along the top of the cups. Poppers at the crotch. I must have bought this sometime around 2004. Pretty sure I've only worn it once. (Oh yes, that memory has come bounding back -dirty weekend, older man. Oh dear, get back in your trunk, memory). The reason I don't wear this now is, oh dear, it's a thong back, it's very short in the body, and I'm having flashing images right now about the flabby belly that would just wobble out the sides and...thong? And crotch-poppers? Heck, no.

38C Nude/Black

Another one from Victoria's secret. This time, their 'Very Sexy' range. Not padded, underwired. The front part where the bow is normally placed has a crisscross corset type lacing -nude color with black floral lace overlay. Straps are decorated with lace -very pretty. It's too small for me now, but I used to wear this a lot. It has matching undies, too. (The dog hasn't found them yet).

42D Black

Underwired, not padded. Black lace. Again, looks very pretty. It's from M&S, I think? Holding this one up, it looks too compact and squished together. It's a balconette, so I think my boobs spill over the top of this one. Very 'bodice-ripping' but not very suitable when you're at work or running for the bus. That's black eye material, right there.

38D Blue/Grey

This is one I've had a long while, probably from the nineties, from the look of it. This was one of my favourites back in the day. It's sort of a petrol-blue color with a grey lace overlay. I'm probably not giving it much justice. Underwired, not padded, I think it's a balconette -too small now. And it's not a tee-shirt bra, so you can see the lace through clothes. Perhaps that was a thing back then. I just Googled 'bra lace showing through' -and now need to bleach my eyes.

38D Black

This bra is so old I can't read the ticket, but probably 38D. Black, not padded, underwired. The straps look very decent. I can't remember why I stopped wearing this. The wires seem thin, so I suspect that this one is a 'digger.' (That feeling you get when you get home and the first thing you do is take your bra off?) Yep, this would be that bra.

38D Grey

Not padded, pretty, linear lace in the cups and a pink bow in front. Straps are decorated with lace. Balconette style. However, the straps are thin, and they don't adjust enough, so this one ended up feeling like you were wearing a bra made out of chicken wire. Also, when I hold this one up it looks absolutely tiny. Like, a 32A! (not that I would ever know) I think I wore this once. Extremely uncomfortable. Makes you want to kick a puppy.

36C Multi/Yellow Leopard

This is a very silly, slutty little one. Underwired, front fastening, racer-back, extremely stretchy-lace in a really slutty print. Only looks like a 32. Looks tiny again, but it's extremely stretchy, which is probably why I bought it. The underwires are super-bendy. The cups are all wrong. I suppose this might be okay as a bralette (something I would never go outside in). I was probably entertaining my 'horny teenager' self when I bought this. Haven't seen her since -thank goodness.

42D Black

This one looks like something you could carry your groceries in and is absolutely the most massive bra I have ever seen! Really, you could put wheels on one of the cups and make it into a baby-stroller. It's padded, underwired, and gigantic. The wire in the right cup has snapped in two, and one of the pieces of metal is sticking through. Ah, I remember this one now. The 'snap' happened to me at work one day, so I had to finish my working day with a raw snapped piece of metal stabbing my right boob for several hours. I was gnarly, that day, I can tell you. However, this *was* one of my absolute-favorite bras. Aside from the cups looking huge, the straps are really nice and wide -and padded! My favorite work bra. I really have to throw this in the trash, but I'm wondering whether I can re-purpose the cups into cat beds.

42C Black

This one was from a multipack. It looked super pretty in the pictures. Underwired, not padded. Stretchy lace. I did wear the white version of this for a spell; however, the straps are like shoelaces -absolutely tiny, and they warp very easily. Actually, what I mean there is that they sort of curl up to resemble actual shoelaces. It's the whole gala-melon-shoelace scenario again. Which is a shame because this was a really nice summer bra. If the straps were wider, this would have been perfect.

42C White

I don't own too many white bras. This one is called 'Lottie.' Quite pretty, un-padded, and underwired -nice lace straps. It has interesting details at the front where the bow normally is. It looks like I've never worn this. Probably because the cups are narrower than I'd like – they make my boobs look long and thin. Weird!

42C White

This is the white version of a previous mention. I wore this quite a lot actually, shoelace straps aside – until the straps got so bad, they'd just roll off my shoulders. I should throw this one out really. It's over-laundered, so the white has gone grey, and it looks just plain nasty now. I really must attack my underwear drawer (possibly with a blowtorch).

38D White

Underwired and padded. I bought this from a clothing section of a grocery store one summer. Thought it was pretty because it has cotton broderie-anglaise on the cups and looked very, sort of 'Daisy Duke.' I've cut the ticket out so I'm guessing the size. (Did I mention my ticket-cutting phase?)

When I got this one home and tried it on, I found probably one of the most bizarre issues I've ever had with a bra: I looked down and saw all this extra fabric in the nipple area, which made my boobs look ULTRA pointy. Like the robot women in Austin Powers – you know, where guns pop out.

'Pew! Pew! Pew!' – said the boobies.

I could literally grab the extra fabric. Other than that, it was a really nice bra, fitted nicely, and was comfortable.

I did a few more 'Pew! Pew's' in the mirror before putting this one away (probably forever, unless I meet someone who has a strange Austin Powers fetish).

42C Black

Moulded cups, memory foam, I think. It has pretty lace sides, and fairly decent straps; although, they look like they might not adjust as much as I'd like them to (and which is the most common reason in the 'drawer of doom'). I think this one is identical to my number one 'best bra ever.' The wire snapped on *that* one, so maybe I'll give this another test drive.

42E White

Again, this is one that needs to be thrown out. Extremely old. 42E? Really? I can guarantee that I *wasn't* a 42E when I bought this. What was I thinking? Good lord. It's greyed, which is how I know its old, so I must have worn this a lot. Lovely, padded straps. One of the underwires is entirely missing. So, we've got one underwired cup and one wireless cup. I'm really never going to wear this again. (Remind me to pInterest '101 uses for old bras').

42C Jade Green

Part of a multipack, so I might have already talked about this one. It's the most beautiful bright jade-green color, I really love the color. Underwired, not padded. Not too much hardware in the front and lovely straps. I think this is the 'squashes boobs together' multi-pack. I would only wear this if I was ultra-tired, so I could rest my chin on my boob cushion.

42C Nude/Black

My all-time favorite bra found two years ago. The best one I've ever bought, the king-of-kings, bra from heaven. I wore this forever and would still be, if it were not broken. It's called a 'youthful lift' bra from a well-known department store. I just could not fault this bra in any way. I was devastated when I broke it. It was everything I'd want in a bra. Invisible (never felt it while on), 'lightweight' in front, well enclosed wires. Super-comfortable. And didn't feel like you were wearing something from the Dark ages. Inevitably, I snapped one of the wires, and cried into my coffee for the rest of the week. The department store I bought it from messed about with the design and called it something else, I think. I'm still mourning. I'll have to make a bra-shrine for this one.

44F Black

What? Am I insane? Quite possibly the biggest bra I own (and have ever seen). This must have been a drunk-mail-order thing; it must have been. Was I on a quest to buy every single size of bra? Do I have bra OCD? This could be a cat-carrier. It's a multi-way bra with massive, moulded, ultra-round spherical cups, like a football cut in half. When I put this on my boob, I can grab a handful of extra fabric. My boobs just disappear in it. It has a tiny back-band, and it doesn't look 44. Perhaps I just wanted to own a multi-way bra. Because you know, every woman needs a multi-way bra. I feel like Miss Trunchbowl in this. Oh dear.

Still, got a hammock for the garden next summer.

* * *

So, yeah. I own thirty-four bras in six assorted sizes. My life-long dieting and weight fluctuations are largely responsible for this vast selection. However, bra-style aside, they all have their eccentricities: straps too thin, front too bulky, weird shape, not enough strap adjustment, bad or flimsy wire encasement, smushing cups.

I *should* return any bra that doesn't fit or feel right and say so. I really should – because unless we give this information to manufacturers or buyers, we're going to get much more of the same. Forever.

C is for

Cafés

I recently went out to London for the day as a treat with my sister and my best friend. I work in London, but rarely get to do the 'touristy bit' and since my bestie and I had lost forty pounds each that year, it was first class all the way.

Our first stop after a 'blue-seat' ride on the train, was Simpsons in The Strand. The restaurant was beautiful, old-world oak-paneled and chandeliered (not even sure that's a word) and we were directed to a booth seat.

'Oh, shit.'

On approach to said booth, I could see that there was about eight inches of space between the table and the 'arm' of the booth.

'Double shit.'

Well, it's a blessing that we had both lost so many pounds each; otherwise, we wouldn't have managed to squeeze into the booth. Still, I had to do this weird 'leg thing' over the arm of the bench, sit down and drag my other leg over the top; it was not so elegant, I can tell you, -akin to climbing over a gate in a field.

So, there we were, enjoying our jolly posh surroundings, and it suddenly dawned on me that there was just no way I was going to get *out* of this booth. The booths and table, as I had suspected, were wall-fixed and immovable. I was going to have to do the 'leg thing' again, and I hoped the party of twelve at the adjacent table would be gracious enough not to notice me doing a 'Bear Grylls' to get out of my booth.

My best friend is a beautiful, bubbly type of lady who just doesn't let anything like that bother her. However, I was silently mortified all through breakfast. Luckily, the people at the table settled their bill and left and, since we were having quite a late breakfast, there was no one else coming in.

Staff were beginning to set the tables for lunch, and I waited until they had gone back into the kitchen to do my 'Bear-Grylls leg-swing.' It was truly ugly – I kind of swung my left leg over the top of the bench, did a twist, hopped a couple of steps back, and dragged my other leg over the top. I'm quite sure my bestie did it in a far more elegant way.

I, however, left the restaurant wishing I'd insisted on a table and chairs in the centre of the room, rather than a booth. Maybe then I would have spent the time enjoying my Eggs Florentine, instead of wondering how I was going to escape elegantly. Another reason I don't wear skirts.

On the same day, we ended up in the Godiva Chocolate café in Harrods. As a treat (we'd been weight-watching ALL year), we ordered a ton of stuff, and the two immaculately-turned-out young ladies at the table next to us went completely silent when our order arrived.

Every time either of us picked up a fork, they stopped talking and elbowed each other to look over.

It took all my willpower not to make a scene. I cast glances sideways at them to see their sniping looks at each other. I find it really difficult not to be self-conscious, I don't have thick skin in these situations. Part of me wants to explain myself to these strangers, so that they don't just go away back to work and tell their colleagues about the two fatties stuffing cake at the next table.

It shouldn't matter to me at all what these other immaculate and beautiful brunching-ladies were thinking. (I'm working on that).

In the meantime, I will stick to my regular little Italian Coffee shop. The owner is a lovely old Italian man who sneaks amaretto into my expresso on weekends. Also, he's re-modelled and changed his bloody awful chairs.

Chair's that, every time I sat in them, would make me visualize myself standing up walking away with a chair stuck to my arse.

It never happened, thankfully.

Calories

Here's what I learned about calories. A calorie is a unit of energy that the body requires to function. Breathing, blinking, sitting, sleeping, reading this (which hopefully requires a few brain cells to be firing) – and everything else that makes us alive – requires calories.

The rate at which an individual burns these calories at rest is known as their Base Metabolic Rate (BMR).

We get calories from food. Calories not used up are stored in a particular type of cell: A fat cell. The scientific name for a fat cell is an 'adipocyte.'

1lb (0. 45kg) of fat = 3500 calories. (One billion fat cells).

An average human adult has 30 billion fat-cells with a weight of 30 lbs.

Control of calorie intake (or lack of) is how the human body gets fat, or thin. Not understanding this, does not mean that it doesn't apply; I suspect this is the part that the diet industry hopes I only vaguely understand, so that they can sell me their 'amazing miracle diets.' – it worked for more decades than I'd care to divulge. Mostly out of embarrassment.

I also calculated that if I am ten pounds (4. 5kg) overweight, it means that I have consumed, and am carrying 35,000 excess calories which equates to ten billion fat-cells.

Therefore, being one hundred pounds (45. 35kg) overweight, it means that I have consumed, and am carrying 350,000 excess calories. I don't know how many fat-cells that is; my calculator doesn't display that many zeros.

Every individual human being has a base calorie requirement. That is to say...to be a living, functioning human being requires a certain daily calorie intake. If I was to lie on a bed for an entire day and not move, I would still burn calories. So, let's say, I need two-thousand calories just to be alive, to be here writing this book. This is my 'ZERO' ladies (and gents). It is known as 'Basal ('Base') Metabolic Rate' or 'BMR.'

At my heaviest, I was carrying an extra hundred pounds. That means that I had stored up enough calories to survive for 175 days without food. Almost six months. (Assuming a BMR of 2000 calories). Of course, I would die much sooner from dehydration.

In order to lose this, I would have to consume less than my BMR so that my body goes looking for fat cells (which are everywhere, probably even on my eyelids) – to make up the shortfall.

On a typical day, I'd start with your BMR as a minus, this is what I basically need to get through a day before I've so much as blinked. Let's call this my bank. And you start overdrawn. In the context of losing weight, being overdrawn is a great thing.

To stay the same weight, I'd basically eat up to 'zero.' To lose weight, my BMR bank is going to have to stay overdrawn. As a result, my body looks to my fat to find the calories I need.

* * *

Here's the math I learned:

Let's assume my BMR is 2000 and I want to *lose* 1lb (0. 45kg) in a week:
 -2000 calories (bank overdrawn) -2, 000
 +1500 calories (put calories in, eat) -500
 +500 calories (burned from fat) = 0
 (I've used up 3,500 calories from my fat cells: 1lb)

In short, there are two important things I need to do when aiming to lose weight. One, calculate my own personal BMR and two, eat less than that.

Cambridge Diet (Review)

I haven't tried this (some review, hey). I believe that Cambridge was one of the first types of meal-replacement diets. I remember a friend of mine doing it in the eighties, although can't remember having any strong feelings about it, one way or another, other than I thought it sounded boring.

See 'Lighter Life' - this is a similar meal replacement program, and includes an astonishing interview.

Catfishing

See X-Rated

Change

Mindset: noun: The established set of attitudes held by someone.

I've learned that in order to get to my weight goal or maintain it, I'm going to have to learn what got me there in the first place and to acknowledge that. Then change my attitude towards my nutrition.

I have a very petulant attitude towards food. It's really very childish. For me, my subconscious voice says, I'm gonna eat that, and no one can stop me. I earned it, it's mine. I deserve it.

This is my mindset. As such, I need to re-program my brain to say something else.

Mindset (attitude) shouldn't be confused with habit, though you could say that I've repeatedly said these things to myself, much like a habit. A habit has more to do with a physical situation that is learned through repetition.

For instance: I might be used to getting home and plonking in front of the telly/computer with four rounds of cheese on toast every night. I've made this a habit, like brushing my teeth.

Changing an attitude is difficult. To me, an attitude is part of my identity. I think I need to go back in my life and try and discover how this attitude was formed.

Perhaps, growing up as the oldest of three siblings meant that I didn't always have what I wanted. Now, living alone, and earning my own money has made me free to nurture the attitude that I can have whatever I want, without consequence (I've since learned this is not *necessarily* bad).

This, for me, is the most terrifying aspect of losing weight. When I think about doing something different in this context, I feel quite fearful.

I get a sort of mental block when I consider what's going to have to change in order for me to change my mindset. It feels like I'm exiting a comfort zone into a world that I am unfamiliar with, and this will be one of the hardest things to change for me.

So, let's put this in the real world. I've stopped getting home from work and eating cheese-on-toast in front of the telly. Let's say I make a salad instead. If I haven't changed my mindset, my brain is going to get petulant.

'Pfff, wish this was cheese on toast,' or Sad face,

'I miss my cheese on toast: $^$'£$% salads!'

And so on. The danger is that all the time I am eating salad, my brain is still being petulant., and there's an outside chance I'll finish my salad and *then* go make cheese on toast. This is because my attitude towards food hasn't changed.

After that time, it's likely there's a 'beat myself up' period, which puts me in a position where I'll seek comfort in, well, *more* cheese on toast.

Changing a mindset (attitude) requires preparation, repetition, and tools to help me during times when I have these thoughts or attitudes. I've also learned that mindfulness can help in these situations.

See Mindfulness

Change One Thing

One really nifty tool that I learned, somewhere during my endless dieting escapades, is the 'change one thing' concept.

As it sounds, it's about changing *one* thing (not a scary prospect) and forming it into a habit. That is, to make a new neural pathway, strengthen it by repetition, and make the old pathway weaker or non-existent altogether.

It's a gentle and very slow way to change a habit, forever. Once my mindset (attitude) is on its way to changing, I list things in my diet that need to change. These need to be very small, single things. Like this:

- Sugar in my coffee
- Butter on bread
- Full fat mayo
- Not enough vegetables
- Buying candy on the way to work
- Cake day at work
- Taking a lift to go up one floor

I pick one of these and make it my mission, for at least a month, to change it, until it becomes a habit (something we automatically do). Once it's well established, I tick it on the list and add another.

For my mind, this is a very non-shocking way to change eating habits. I practice this a lot (my list is long...). I always remember to make sure that the list contains single things, not great sweeping statements like 'become a marathon runner'.

Cheating

Cheating refers to the breaking of rules to gain advantage in a [competitive] situation.

In the context of committing to weight loss, this seems to be a bit of a misnomer, doesn't it? What advantage am I giving myself when I'm 'on a diet' and I stop for takeout on the way home from work? I think what I mean by cheating here, is this sort of thing:

- Getting takeout on the way home after being weighed
- Not eating on the day preceding a weigh-in
- Not going to weigh-in class because I 'fell off the wagon.'
- Spend a day in a sauna, wrapped in plastic before a weigh day?

It's the wrong word to use, isn't it? I should call it self-sabotage, shouldn't I? It's really difficult to suggest a remedy for these things I do, since everyone is different. Mindset and mindfulness can most likely address these things too. Something in my mind has definitely changed lately, and I can't quite put a finger on it.

Several months ago, while travelling home from work, I'd be thinking of getting takeout, for one 'reason' or another. I'd get in my car and drive towards the store. And then, I'd drive on past and go home. It almost felt like I was scoping out a bank to rob. But I patted myself on the back, nonetheless. This kept happening for a few weeks, until I just went straight home after work. Essentially, I stopped 'scoping out the bank'.

I think, for me, I kept driving because I couldn't face 'my inner voices' the next morning. (see Mood Swings). So, I won that episode of inner conflict. A devil on one shoulder saying,

'Come on, let's get takeout, no one else will know'

While the angel on the other shoulder floors my accelerator, saying,

'No, no, no, let's go home and have a lovely candle-lit bath instead.'

My angel won, and keeps winning lately, I'm pleased to say.

If I'm tempted to 'cheat', I try and recognise what caused the thought and prepare for it. I practice in thought how I am going to deal with these situations. I practice until the neural pathway to 'cheat' has me doing something else entirely, other than actually 'cheating'.

See also Habits

Clothing Sizes

Why is it that there isn't some kind of Law or British Standard that governs clothing sizes?

A long diet ago, I remember a lady weighing me while I was saying (all positive and happy), 'I got into a size twenty today!' to which she replied, 'A twenty from where?'

What she actually meant was, each clothing store has a different size twenty. Either way, she pissed on my parade. She was dead-right, though.

Donkeys-years ago, most clothing stores (okay, less choice then) were very similar with their sizes. A size ten was the same, store to store. So was a twelve. So was a fourteen (I know this because I was all of those sizes in the eighties). In fact, I don't remember that much difference in the early nineties either.

Somehow, somewhere along the line, it all went pear-shaped.

These days, two size-twenty items in the same store fit differently. Two different blouses in the same store, for instance. Both have sleeves and a seam where the sleeve is sown on. Both are similar fabric. I'll try one on and it fits nicely; I'll try on another and it's too tight in the arms. I could wear it, but I wouldn't be able to hug my boyfriend without doing a 'David Banner.'

Could the clothing industry aspire to some minimum standards? The British sizing system hasn't changed since the fifties. Until then, I'll continue to buy my max-stretch jersey clothes and elasticated waists.

Count

Another nifty little tool that I find really helps at times when I'd normally be grabbing cookies, is to count.

I counted ten breaths (in, one, out, two); every time I thought about going to the fridge/freezer/biscuit tin, I'd then reach for, or do something else, instead.

For instance, wash hands, put on some hand cream, cuddle the cat, drink water, make some green tea. Just something else that was positive and kind.

Actually, this is a great mini meditation: to be still for a count.

I make sure I have alternatives things to do around me at all times. If I stick with it, it really helps.

D is for

Dating

See 'X-rated'

Diet

Here's what I've learned.
What is a 'diet'?
In actual fact, a diet is 'what a particular species survives on' or, the official definition according to Wiki:
'the sum of the food consumed by an organism or group'

- Lions exist on a diet of meat. They are carnivores.
- Cows exist on a diet of grass. They are herbivores.
- Spiders exist on a diet of insects. They are insectivores.
- As a species, human beings are Omnivores – this means we eat everything.

It is our culture, group, or regional dietary habits that influence the habitual decisions an individual, or entire culture, make when choosing what foods to eat; and it's our 'dietary habit' that determines what we choose to eat.
So, in fact, it's my *habits* that need to change.
When I talk about diets, I'm talking about a particular eating plan that I am going to adopt -for a set period of time -to a target weight:
'I'm on a diet.'
'Have you tried the doobrey diet?' 'That diet didn't work for me.'
'I lost a hundred pounds on the waffle diet.'
In my opinion, as long as I continue using the word 'diet' it will be this 'thing' that I do, until I get to a target weight, fail, or decide 'it' isn't for me. Then, I'll try another 'thing.'

It's this hook that the diet industry has me dangling on... every time. They target my biggest fears, and make a diet about it:

'Shit, I'm going to be in a bikini next month.' (the bikini diet)

'Oh my gosh, Christmas is coming.' (the Christmas diet)

'Shit, Bob's party next month.' (the Little Black Dress diet)

If you type the most ridiculous thing into Google, there's a diet for it: The Cucumber Diet; the Cabbage Diet; the Donut Diet; the Sex Diet; the Jesus Diet. Yep. They all exist. Note to self: Bookmark, 'The Sex Diet' to read later.

What's common about all of these, is that they all exist to address a temporary concern (except Jesus). They are quick fixes. They don't address why I am the way I am, or teach me to change permanently, or care about what I'll do afterwards.

By that time, they've sold it to me. They have achieved what they wanted to achieve. And, guaranteed, that next year I'll be looking for that Christmas diet again.

So, the diet industry is literally selling my fat arses back to me.

I suspect that if I break these diets down to their bare bones, gimmicks aside, they are all the same: Calorie controlled.

Food for thought.

Face-palm. I know, that was awful.

Diet Pills

I signed up to a diet pill weight loss plan in the late eighties. I went to a flashy, posh clinic in Guildford. I don't remember much about the process, though I must have been weighed at some point and had a consultation with someone.

I remember I had to drink a LOT of water while taking these pills. And I did – way over two liters a day.

A couple of days in, I started waking up in the middle of the night with the most excruciating pains I'd ever experienced. It felt like everything from the waist up, inside, was a dried-up husk, and it HURT.

I instantly believed I was going to die.

One night I got up and walked towards my parents' room, thinking I've really fucked up this time, they're going to be so pissed.

I didn't open the door, though. I can't remember what happened after that, other than I stopped taking the pills immediately and never went back to that 'clinic.' I don't think my parents even had an inkling that I was taking diet pills or had almost died that night.

Since then, I've never gone near any pill that claims to help me lose weight. Aside from full-on surgery, this was probably the most dangerous thing I've ever tried in order to lose weight. I was nineteen at the time. Imagine dying at that age? Ugh.

I'd have missed meeting my best friend; I'd have missed falling in love (many times); I'd have missed the best shag of my life; I'd have missed hugging a Dachshund puppy; I'd have missed so many things. All for weight loss.

I've also learned, according to some medical journals I've read, certain diet pills can cause heart attack and death, as well as varied stomach/intestinal damage.

See Bibliography for these sources.

Doctors

Back when I was seven or eight, I think, my Mother took me to a doctor because I was fat. He measured my height - and that was about all the attention he paid to me. I came away from there feeling like there was something wrong with me, and my mum came away with a prescribed diet for me: half a boiled potato and cabbage as every meal until I was 'right' again.

I felt like I'd let someone down, disappointed someone.

I was great in school; I was on the gymnastics team; I was in the choir; I played instruments; I cared for pets (and a pony actually); I even taught myself to read music. I loved writing, and adored reading. I watched old black and white movies on TV. And I was well behaved with good grades in school.

How is it then that I remember this doctor's visit, but not ever being encouraged in any of the positive things? What it actually left me with was an enduring hatred of boiled potatoes and cabbage. And this might possibly be where my petulance toward food began.

These days, there are news headlines about obesity, and diabetes, and fat people crippling healthcare systems.

All the while, my current Doctor has never raised the subject with me, or any concern about my being so overweight.

She'll happily prescribe me pain killers for chronic back pain (which is caused, I don't doubt, by being overweight). I also take pills for ankle and knee pain (possibly caused or aggravated by being overweight). She sends me on countless blood tests because I have complained on one or two occasions about being tired (probably caused by a bad diet) and has given me antibiotics for a skin condition, which I am sure is aggravated by anxiety, most likely caused by being ashamed of how I look, caused by being fat.

Could it be that this 'skirting around the issue' is aggravating the issue in the first place?

Of course, by the time I am actually fat, being called 'fat' probably has greater implications -not least because my self-esteem is probably suffering at the same time, whether I am consciously aware of this fact or not.

Having low self-esteem is a very dark downward spiral, that requires a very small trigger to send me veering off into depression, agoraphobia, or worse. So, it's at this stage that people tend to refrain from saying these things out loud. There are just too many complications about being fat, in my opinion. Imagine a great knotted ball of string which is responsible for it. This would have to be unraveled before addressing the excess weight. There's just no black and white about it.

Perhaps that's why general care physicians don't go there -for fear of being accused of fat-shaming, or because they just don't have time to help me unravel the psychological reasons behind my weight.

Surely, it wouldn't hurt for a Doctor to open the conversation in a kind way. The conversation needs to be had, because of all the issues that go along with being overweight, not just the fact that I am.

E is for

Exercise

Over the course of my life, my relationship with exercise has been either one extreme or the other.

In 1993-ish, I made a new year's resolution to quit smoking, lose weight and get fit. I was probably 28-ish pounds overweight back then.

I remember being utterly resolved and removed myself entirely from situations where food might be an issue, or one where I might be encouraged to smoke.

On the first of January I went in to one of our sheds at home (it was frickin' cold in there, I can tell you), set up a TV and a video machine and stuck in the video by Cher entitled 'A New Attitude.' And off I went.

The video is one of my all-time favourites: decent music, everyone is happy and, you know -CHER! I practiced this every single day. I'd get home from work, change into my snazzy leotard, cycle shorts, LA Gear high tops, possibly even a headband...and off I'd go.

A couple of months later, mid-workout, I felt my right lung kind of 'pop' and I realised what had happened...I had quit smoking, and my lung had 'uncrumpled' and inflated back to its normal state. I took a long, deep breath and felt completely elated. I can't explain the feeling, but I was just ecstatic.

By April/May that year, I was completely hooked on exercise. I remember feeling like a sack of wet sand until I'd completed my workout. I refused to do anything, or speak to anyone, until I'd stepped along with Cher.

I still displayed addictive behaviors, though, and hadn't really changed my mindset. I just hid myself away. When I started craving social interaction, it didn't take much coaxing for me to hop in the car, buy a pack of cigarettes, and meet my friends in a pub to drink and eat. That wasn't my friends' fault, it was petulance. And that was the end of that healthy chapter for another ten years.

Everything got in the way after that. My job had me working away, so there were long drives, tiredness, and stress. All I wanted to do in the evenings and weekends was party. Money was another thing. I was earning more, so I felt entitled about partying and treating myself.

I had another 'flaunt' with exercise around 2011 when I hired a personal trainer. One that came to my house and 'beasted' me for an hour. I kind of loved it, but I still hadn't changed my attitude about weight loss. Right after he'd leave, I'd shove my head in the fridge.

He also injured me, albeit semi-permanently. It wasn't his fault. He just didn't have the experience or knowledge about obesity to think that his exercises might permanently damage my joints. I bought into it, though. By the time I cancelled my sessions, I absolutely loved sparring. It was funny to watch me at five-feet tall and him -over six feet -trying to punch his hands.

These days I don't exercise in the conventional sense. I might do a couple of hours of digging in the garden or get off the bus one stop early. I do things that are gentle. Things I don't dread. My joints are more or less screwed, and I don't fancy a wheelchair when I'm sixty.

Most weight-loss classes or plans have a little guidebook, which has tools, tips, suggestions, and a section about exercise. It will display a list of various exercises and how many calories you can 'burn' by doing them.

I learned that these are just guidelines:

Imagine two people at the bottom of a flight of stairs. One is a hundred pounds overweight. The other is a twenty-year-old long-distance runner. It's simply fact that the overweight person is going to burn more calories to get up those stairs. So, it follows that, as I lose weight, I burn fewer calories when exercising. So, I need to do *more* in order to achieve the same weight loss. If I don't, I'll hit a plateau, and stop losing weight.

Another way I look at it is the lighter I get, the more minutes I need to exercise:

A 240-pound person would have to do Pilates for 75 minutes to burn 500 calories. A 120-pound person would have to do Pilates for 150 minutes to burn the same amount.

Most importantly, since I am extremely overweight, my plan is to start slow/short and gentle low impact sessions and build it up over a long term. I'm sure my joints will thank me for it later. Low impact means, basically, that I'm not stressing my joints. Walking, Yoga, Thai-Chi, or Body Groove are excellent to begin with.

For sweating buckets, try Zumba -or if you're feeling like a warrior-goddess: sparring. If you have a partner, have him/her wear the pads. Stand back, enough to (obviously) be able to punch, but not so far that you 'snap' your elbows when you punch. That's what buggered my elbows up. That, and four-minute planks.

Thai-Chi is surprisingly fruitful. You know if you swap the first letters over, you also have a beverage. But don't go ordering a Thai Chi at Starbucks now.

F is for

Falling off the Wagon

I don't really fall off the wagon. It's more of a *'fall off and get dragged behind the wagon for a while'* situation.

I can literally have an almighty epiphany and lose weight sensibly for months, but then I'll have, say, a week off over Christmas where I allow myself some un-counted days – then the week turns into a couple of weeks, and getting back on the wagon becomes difficult.

Its then when the excuses start rolling in:

- *'I'll start next week.'*
- *'I have stayed the same so I'm okay'*; and ultimately,
- *'I can handle this on my own.'*

I wonder sometimes if I'm ever going to learn that I just can't, and of course by the time I do, I'll have put on all the weight I lost. My best friend started her weight loss before me, had the same time off at Christmas, and then, unlike me, got straight back on the wagon.

She's now a size sixteen, which is awe-inspiring. Last time we met; her resolve convinced me to do something about my weight.

A few weeks in, I felt amazing. I felt that something had truly changed in my mind – I lost almost forty pounds. And then…I fell off that wagon.

I fell off that wagon even after I bought some pants and cried *because they fit*.

I fell off that wagon even after doing a double take at myself in a mirror because my belly had shrunk so dramatically.

I fell off that wagon even after I'd fly up a flight of stairs and not be out of breath at the top.

Why, why, why?

A hypnotherapist once told me that I'd taught my brain that 'failing is normal.' Since then, I've read other books about how the brain works and how habits are formed, which I'll cover briefly in another chapter.

Fatigue

When she was quite overweight, my best friend used to sleep a lot. I just couldn't understand it – until I was more overweight than she was.

I remember that, if she parked herself on a sofa for more than four minutes, she'd be asleep – wherever we were. My house, her house, or another friend's house. She'd apologize *while* she was asleep.

'I'm sorry' she'd say, 'Was I snoring?'

She's so adorable, honestly. Since then, I've learned that fatigue is pretty unavoidable if you are very overweight with a not-so-great diet and a bad eating-schedule.

I learned that if I satisfy those calories with high sugar and high carbohydrates at the wrong times, the desire to sleep is ravenous.

I've always been a light 'breakfaster': coffee and maybe a banana was all I could manage in the morning.

On weekends, I'd get home and make myself a lunch (like a great big tuna-mayo pasta) and by 2 p. m. I could barely keep my eyes open. I've scared myself, on more than one occasion, with the feeling that comes over me.

It feels unnatural; it feels like some adverse biological reaction. I feel so weak I can barely walk; it's like my body wants to completely shut down.

So, I sleep. I used to sleep on a Saturday afternoon. I'd call them 'naps' -as if they were little naughty, luxurious treats.

The reality was that they were huge, exhausting, four-hour sleeps.

I'd set my alarm clock, in all honesty because I felt guilty *and* was afraid that I wouldn't wake up. That's a bit warped, isn't it? If I died, I'm not going to un-die when the alarm goes off. Silly mare.

I'd wake up feeling terrible, like I'd come down off some drug and I'd crave something fresh and cold, like water, fresh air, fruit juice, or cold milk to wake me up inside. I'd often have a headache and feel weak for at least an hour. And then I'd beat myself up emotionally because it all just felt so wrong.

Nothing luxurious about that, is there?

At one point, I visited my doctor and told her about it. She sent me to the hospital for all kinds of blood tests and nothing turned up.

At the moment, things have improved. With a much more sensible diet (next-to-no bread or pasta -by choice) I feel much less of a need to be asleep. When I feel like I could 'nap' I drink some water and have a piece of fruit, or I get up and do something -even if it's watering my garden or sorting my knicker-drawer (seventy-four pairs, last count); I achieve something instead. I still feel tired, I suppose – even right now.

But it's not that frightening, overwhelming feeling that I want to sleep for a week. Go, me.

Fat Lumps

Also known as Lipomas (I dare you to YouTube it).

These are lumps of fat under the skin that I've notice appear more when I'm heavier. Mine are tiny compared to the ones I've seen on the internet. I have about four of them on my forearms, and a couple on my lower back. They feel like lumps of gristle and can be painful if I accidentally knock them.

I mentioned one to my doctor years ago. She felt it and explained that I could get them removed if they are bothering me, but they are totally harmless.

I'd far rather waste my doctors time and have her say, 'Eh, it's nothing' than worry about the lump and stew about it being something sinister.

I do remember when I phoned to make that appointment I mentioned 'lump' and was seen within half an hour. So, ya know, bonus.

Fat-Shaming

Pillory: verb (used with object), pilloried, pillorying. to expose to public derision, ridicule, or abuse.

Thoughtless remarks stick in my mind, forever. It's just how I'm wired. It hurts too. I want to share some of the comments sent my way over the years that I have never forgotten. Take from them what you will:

* * *

1978 ish – I was 8. Doctors visit about being fat. (See Doctors)

* * *

1982 ish – I was 12. A friend and I were walking to the bus stop for school. Halfway there, she said to me, 'Walk ahead of me a minute.' So, I did. She giggled and said, 'You walk funny!'
   I felt mortified. It stuck with me ever since.

* * *

2010 ish – I was at a pub/restaurant with my dad, sister, and her fiancé. After the main meal, Fiancé and I go out for a cigarette and while we we're outside one of his old friends happened to come by.

The old male-back-slapping ensued, and they talked a brief catch up. Then, looking to me and back to Fiancé, the friend said, 'And, is this your girlfriend?'

My Sisters fiancé sort of leaned back suddenly (as if backing away from an unpleasant smell, or losing balance) and said,

'NO! No, my girlfriend is inside.'

(I could swear he almost said, 'Oh fuck, NO').

But that split-second look of horror on his face, I will never forget. He's a pleasant chap, and I'm absolutely sure he didn't realise that I'm so adept at picking up micro-expressions, but there you are.

* * *

2010 ish – I was in a grocery store and a lady with a toddler walked by, 'Mummy look at the fat lady, Mummy!' She ushered her toddler past me with a semi-amused look on her face. Had I retaliated, I'd have come off as neurotic.

* * *

1998 ish – I was in the kitchen at home, and I'd opened a pack of lemon slices (like, finger cakes). There were eight in the box. I stood at the window and ate one or two. Then I saw my Dad walking across the yard towards the house, I remember thinking, I wonder how many I can eat before he gets here, and so, I ate them all, in the twenty or so strides it took him to get to the house.

Not a fat-shaming incident really. I can't remember why I had that thought, or why I did it. It's just stuck with me. Possibly because Dad's sense of humor was to creep up behind me when I was eating and shout, 'WHATYOUEATING!'

It was fun to him, and I totally get that. I love my dad more than anyone in the entire world. But I think it had an effect on me because he'd say it whenever he saw me eating.

He doesn't do that at all now really, but still, I avoid eating in front of him. I don't consider that his fault at all, though.

FAT-SHAMING

* * *

2011 ish - You know those kinds of people who just keep saying worse things as they're trying to dig themselves out of a hole? Well, this was that night...

I was in Florida with a boyfriend, and we frequented the Pensacola Fish House as regularly as we could afford. Right on the ocean, the food was just spectacular -would leave me speechless. So beautiful. On this particular night, we had a little table for two by the window at the back of the restaurant. We were greeted by a lady I hadn't seen there before, and I should have known something was up when she literally looked me up and down when we walked in. She had this excessively cheerful manner that felt aggressive. My instincts were put on alert, know what I mean?

We were ushered to the bar to wait for our table, and we were in fine form -both happily chatting away, ordering drinks, and talking about our day. It was beautiful evening; you could smell a fresh ocean breeze and it had just started to cool down. I was enjoying a grey goose and tonic -with lime, of course.

All of a sudden, this face appeared from behind me, almost rested on my shoulder. 'My, how did you get up there?' referring to the bar stool. (I'm five feet tall).

It was her. I sort of frowned at her and looked at my boyfriend. I supposed I should've laughed. Before I could say anything, 'Table's ready! Careful getting down from there -follow me!'

And off she went. We followed, having sat at the same table before, we knew where we were going.

Then she stopped dead in her tracks in front of two tables of eight: sixteen people total. Our seat was beyond those two tables, and on several nights prior we just walked between them. No problem.

Tonight, this woman went up and stood in between both tables, 'Excuse me everyone -sorry to disturb your meals' she began, in a loud, clear voice, 'But this lady needs to get through; could you all just stand up and pull your chairs in?' I about fainted. I'd never been so utterly mortified in all my life. I shut my eyes briefly and saw eight people stop eating, look at me and stand up. I rushed through to our table and sat down.

Then my jaw dropped, and my boyfriend noticed. 'Don't make a scene; please don't embarrass me' he said.

I'm pretty fierce. He knew that. But out of respect for him, I just remained jaw-dropped for a minute or two. I was apoplectic. (always wanted to use that word).

My reverie was interrupted by the same woman, 'Now, drinks? More drinks? Are we having appetizers? Of course, we are. Two appetizers? Three? What can I get you?'

I blinked slowly. The urge to retaliate was palpable. 'Just the crab cakes -we share. Thank you' I replied.

'Oh, just one? Why not have one each I -"

'No, just one.' My boyfriend gave me a cautionary look and shook his head very subtly, as if to say don't.

She was gone. Throughout the first two courses, every time I looked up, she was staring at me. She definitely knew she'd ruined my evening.

After the second course (mine was Jack Daniels Chicken Salad, beautiful), she came back and sidled up, taking a chair next to my boyfriend. Could this be an apology? She had two dessert menus in hand. Looking right at me she said, 'So, you like chocolate, right?'

Okay, no, that wasn't an apology.

'No.'

'How about a nice big piece of chocolate cake? Everyone likes chocolate.'

'No.' She handed me the dessert menu. Not my boyfriend. Me.

'We'll just have a key lime pie with two forks.'

I refused the menu and left her holding it out towards me. I didn't look at her. 'Thank you' I said, as if to say, 'Make like a tree, you old cow.'

When she returned with the key lime pie, she also had a plate of chocolate cake. 'On the house.' She was going to put it in front of me, and my boyfriend took it. He knew that if she'd come any closer with her 'apology' it would have been shoved in her face.

Neither of us could finish a dessert each. My boyfriend sat back in his chair as he was stuffed. That was a signal for the heifer to come back.

FAT-SHAMING

'All done?' She looked at me, 'Want a doggy bag?'

While my boyfriend was pulling out his credit card I stood up, made an excuse about needing some air, and swept out of there.

I'd never experienced so much passive aggression in all my life and haven't since.

Spectacular food, though.

* * *

2011 ish - This isn't really a fat-shaming story, but it's a bit of a carry-on moment, which deserves a mention.

At that particular time, I was attending 'Lighter Life' classes. This is basically a meal-replacement diet, where you have three shakes a day and a granola bar type thing.

I was at the grocery store at the time, somewhere I did not need to be since Lighter Life provided all my meals. I can't remember what I went to the store for, but I do remember that I had a trolley, and it had food in it.

I was walking up the bread aisle, which also happens to be the cake aisle, when I see another 'Lighter Life' class member coming towards me - her trolley full of food.

It was a classic moment. I'm sure the moment we clapped eyes on each other we were thinking of a valid reason to be in the cake aisle at a time when we didn't need to be buying groceries at all.

It was a moment where it would be worse if you turn around and walk the other way, so we awkwardly greeted each other. It was hilarious.

'Oh, Hi! How are you! I was just, erm, buying some groceries for my Father who can't get out of the house' she said, as if she'd just been caught spraying graffiti.

We were both trying to subtly see what was in each other's trolleys. We made some idle chit-chat, and then carried on with our day (really, we couldn't get away from each other fast enough). I can't help chuckling when I remember that. Of all the people, in all the cake aisles, in all the world, she had to walk down mine. I wasn't even in that aisle for cake, but we both subconsciously agreed that it was pointless explaining.

She didn't show up at the weigh-in that week.

* * *

2017 - I went out to my car and had discovered that someone had parked so close to my car that I couldn't open the door. I could barely squeeze down the side to the door, and since my car doors are so very 'thick' I'd never have even opened it.

I asked another neighbor if they knew whose car it was, and they pointed to a neighbor about six doors down from me.

I went to his door, knocked, and this is how the conversation went,

'Hello, I—'

'Oh yes, you're the Mercedes lady! I'm parked next to you aren't I!'

'Yes, umm, I can't get into my ca—'

'Parked a bit too close, aren't I? Yes, I remember it being a bit of a squeeze,'

'Well, is it possible that you ca—'

'I'd imagine you can't get into your car then; it was a struggle for me, but then I'm a lot thinner than you'

'Uh, I—'

'One minute, I'll come out and move my car for you, eh?'

I sat in my car and cried for about ten minutes. Then

I was really pissed. It ended up as being not his fault for parking so close that I needed a CAN opener, but my fault because I was fat? That wasn't my fault. You're supposed to use your eyes to park a car, mate, not 'The Force.'

* * *

2017 – Is there such a thing as 'reverse fat shaming'?

A while ago at work, one of the Big bosses posted on the internal company web site (the 'intranet') that he's lost a lot of weight, simply by using the NHS's advice – eat less and move more. He explained that there weren't any magic tricks or miracle cures.

I remember thinking, 'Good on you, sir.' And he's dead-right.

One of the responses to this, was from a bloke who said something along the lines of,

'Well done, I'm a life-long exerciser and qualified personal trainer. There's a ton of other fat people in this building and they really need to do something about it.'

Well, a rabid uproar ensued (in a very polite, 'corporate' way).

Many people called this guy 'rude', and others were more diplomatic, saying, 'Well, if you're qualified, you'll know very well that there are many reasons and personal circumstances for being overweight.'

I took a step back from being involved in the 'public' conversation. Well, this was on the Company intranet, so it wasn't public-public; however, I decided to send the guy a private email.

I explained that, whilst I acknowledge what he was trying to say, to look at someone who is overweight and assume they are just fat, lazy over-eaters (and doing nothing about it) is a bit harsh, and to understand that they might already be doing something about it.

I lost forty pounds last year, for instance, but having so much more weight to lose, you wouldn't think that if you'd just met me, you'd just see a fat person.

I sent the email in support of this guy's comments in a way (against my better judgement of wanting to say, 'Fuck you'). I ended the email by asking that, when he next looks at someone who is fat, try and imagine that they might already be doing something about it, or that there might be something else (medically) going on.

The response I expected was something along the lines of Thank you for your response, or no response at all (since, in a very polite way, I was asking him to change his view).

The response I got (and I kid you not) was,

'I don't expect to come to work and be pilloried and harassed. I'm seeking legal advice for bullying. I don't come to work to feel unsafe. I didn't say anything about 'overweight' people.'

(Well, he did), but I didn't respond to this. I think I went into shock.

Woah there, sparky. Overreact, much?

I've never been accused of bullying before. Was I just accused of harassment because I tried to defend myself?

If this was a conversation about someone who was gay, black, yellow, or physically impaired, this guy would have been fired immediately and marched off the premises. Or at the very least, officially disciplined.

There's no 'protection' for someone who is overweight, as it's commonly viewed as a self-inflicted condition, so we're fair game. I'm not being a rabid activist here; I don't expect any protection. But I do want to be able to respond to someone calling me fat without the standard, corporate-response whine, 'Now you're bullying me.'

When did it become so unacceptable to disagree with someone's opinion?

On the upside, I learned a new word that day.

Fear

I'm a few months into losing weight properly and sensibly now, and next week I'll be the lowest weight I've been in about eight years. I'll be at a size where I can walk into several more dress shops and buy clothes off the rack. My back aches less; I can look after myself a lot easier, and I can walk places. I've even been looking at dresses, boots, and things I've never even contemplated for at least eight years. The other day, I was browsing clothes on the internet and

I felt a sudden stab of panic. Being super fat has been my baseline for so long, I've gotten used to it.

I've gotten used to seeing the look of panic on a man's face when the last available seat on the train is the one next to me. I've gotten used to weird looks when I eat in public. I've gotten used to toddlers in supermarkets saying,

'Look, mommy that fat lady!'

I can, more or less, wear what I like now because no one looks at me.

I wonder what it will be like to be noticed (or NOT be noticed because I'm just 'not extraordinary'). I think I am actually afraid. I can't explain the emotion any other way. I also wonder if that fear slows down my weight loss. I can do this; I know I can. Yet something deep in my unconscious is saying, 'Whoa there, sparky, are you SURE?'

My new mantra for the next month will be to look in the mirror and say, 'Yes, I am sure. Yes, I really AM doing this. And yes, I can.' I must get these semi-negative feelings out of the way.

Femininity

When I go over a certain weight, I completely lose my sense of feminine. The picture I'm trying to paint is not one of flowery dresses, lacy underwear, makeup, and heels, or even submissiveness, but one that fundamentally sits within the soul. This is different for everyone I suppose but this is how it affects me.

Moving in a 'feminine' way becomes difficult. I don't mean 'catwalk' and I don't mean floating like Cinderella with bluebirds. I just mean moving gently and elegantly.

The reality is that it's just walking, but because I'm so fat that my knees won't ever touch and I'm likely to become out-of-breath easily. I may compensate for having a huge overhanging belly by leaning back slightly, and my arms sit slightly outwards because of upper-arm and back fat. This might cause some back pain, and as I'm out of shape because I'm too scared to go to the gym, I'll be out of breath. If I'm in a skirt, my legs will rub and chafe until they are bleeding and sore and I am miserable.

The last thing on my mind at that point is femininity; it's simply going home.

What I yearn for is just a vertical outline (so that my side-on shadow doesn't look like I'm hugging a sack of coal), easy, light steps and that almost undetectable hip sway that women naturally have. Just being female.

Although much improved these days, dressing in what you truly like to wear is near impossible. Caring for oneself is an effort. Sometimes it even feels pointless to make an effort, when you feel that no one is looking at you anyway.

Wow, that went depressingly rock-bottom, didn't it? The point I'm trying to make is that I need to take every possible opportunity to revive that feeling of feminine –which is different for everyone.

For me, I get my hair and nails done every two weeks. I drink a double espresso in a favorite tiny artisan Italian cafe (before he's 'officially' open), buy nice underwear, expensive coffee, and the latest Dior-addict lipstick in the latest color, then float home with the shopping bags.

Fluids

I get scratchy every time I read -in some 'diet' or other -that we should 'drink X liters of water every day.' Oh, sod off. Some 'diets' I've seen positively insist that you drink at least two liters a day.

What I learned here, is that too much water (especially a lot at once) – can be very dangerous, if not fatal. My body will tell me when I am thirsty, and I've learned to listen. I did a fair amount of research on 'water intoxication.'

I'm lucky enough to love water. I can't function until I've had a good chug of water in the morning, and I keep bottles of water just about everywhere. My sister doesn't like water. She can't drink it unless its flavored, then again, she's an athlete so she can burn some 1000 calories just by blinking. I'm also very lucky to *not* like soda. The only soda I actually choose is tonic, in vodka (which, the last time I checked, was the lowest calorie spirit).

Many doctors have differing opinions on this subject. Whatever they tell you, though, I would carefully consider your current relationship with fluids. If it works for you, just keep doing that.

If anyone tells you otherwise, flick them in the soft parts.

G is for

Gastric Band

Ah, I've skirted around this subject wondering how to open it. I figure the simplest way is often the best:

I have a Gastric Band. Let me share my experience.

I had severely low self-esteem at the time I started researching the Gastric Band, in 2009. My auntie came with me to see my doctor, who basically said that I wasn't fat enough (I needed to be over a certain weight, despite already being 100 pounds overweight at the time of my visit) or ill enough (I had to have Diabetes and didn't) for a Gastric Band.

I hadn't sobbed so hard in front of a stranger my entire life than on that particular day.

Despite that set back, I still went ahead with the thing privately. I researched for weeks and I found a private company who were offering Gastric Bands for about six thousand pounds.

My auntie (who was also my Godmother) offered to lend me the money. I was earning well by then, so managed to pay her back quickly. I made a video of my pre-op shopping list (as you do when you're a 'YouTuber' – as this was to be my life for at least three months, post-op:

Chewable calcium, chewable vitamins, chewable vitamin-C, chewable B vitamins, Gaviscon, Rennie Deflatine, a smoothie maker, 'smart' scales with body fat BMI monitor, a hand liquidizer, measuring spoons and cups, the Weight Loss Surgery for Dummies book (which should have been called ...IS for Dummies), the Recipes for Life After Weight Loss Surgery book (which I haven't read to this day), the Eating Well After Weight Loss Surgery book (ditto), vanilla whey protein powder, pineapple juice (I have no idea why this specifically, I can't remember), skimmed milk, bottled water, meal replacement drinks, hot chocolate drink sachets, fruit smoothie drinks, sugar-free jelly pots, coffee drinks, dream topping/whipped desserts and non-fat yoghurts.

My first consultancy visit was with a Consultant Surgeon in Southampton, who had a face like a slapped ass, and manners to match. She was utterly uninterested in me, my problems, or my reasons for getting a Gastric Band. She literally sighed before she started talking, and to this day, I don't remember what she said, I just remember wanting to be out of there as quickly as possible.

***

My operation was booked for the 26th of January 2010, and my father drove me up to the hospital in Manchester where I was to have the op. We stayed in a hotel. We arrived at the hospital the next day at 8 a. m. and, after discovering that a 'meal replacement' drink didn't count as liquids (Nil-by-Mouth for 24 hours obviously), I was shifted to being last on the list for that day.

We waited in my hospital room for eight hours. During that time, I was measured for compression stockings and the anesthetist visited. When the time came for my op, I changed into the sexy, backless, cotton gown and was walked down to theatre. I was put onto the operating table and lay there for at least ten minutes, absolutely alert and conscious, while everyone was milling around getting instruments and whatnot. I remember thinking, you had better knock me out right now or I'm walking. There's something very wrong about being awake in an operating room.

After the op, I had to spend the night in the hospital, which I absolutely hated. I hate hospitals. All that artificial heating. I remember Dad coming in and I asked him to open a window. It was so hot and stuffy in there. Not long after he left, a nurse came in and closed the window again. See Epigraph for a post-op pic.

***

The next day I was offered tea and yoghurt and the surgeon came around to see me. Again, I don't remember much about what he said except, 'Your liver was huge!' (They have to lift the liver to get to the stomach where the band is attached). And that I was to be on soup and liquids only for fourteen days. After a month, I'd have to make an appointment for an 'x-ray fill' which is when they inflate the band with fluid to make it 'active.'

The drive back was traumatic. My poor Father had to deal with me yelping whenever he drove over a bump in the road and eventually, we had to stop so that I could take some painkillers for the remainder of the three-hour trip.

***

For a couple of days afterwards, I had severe pain around the shoulders (the gastric area is inflated with gas to perform the keyhole surgery, and the pain was from the gas rising to expel from my body). For three days, I had to inject myself in the stomach with Heparin.

***

A few months on from the operation, on the 6th of March 2010, I re-visited the hospital for my first fill. Called the 'x-ray fill' this is where you stand in front of an x-ray machine, so that the consultant can stick a needle into your band port and fill it with liquid. I felt like I was in The Matrix. I arrived on time. When I was called, the guy didn't say, 'Hello' didn't say, 'How have you been?' Nothing. There was no consultation whatsoever.

After some prodding and poking, I was told that I couldn't have my first fill, as my port (which 'sits' flat in the tissue of your stomach near the surface) had healed sideways so I'd have to have another operation to re-position the port so that it was facing outwards and flat.

***

On the 14th of April 2010, I had another operation to re-position the port. I hated that hospital too and refused to stay the night there. I had just discovered my boyfriend's profile on a dating website, so, you know, not great timing. I was stressed, anxious and hot. I remember that day as bordering an all-out panic attack in the hospital room until my Dad drove for three hours to come and get me.

***

I had my first 'proper' fill on the 3rd of June 2010. I have a 14cc band and it was filled to 7. 5ccs. Post fill, I had to be on liquids for a couple of days, then soft foods (bananas, etc.), and then 'normal' food.

GASTRIC BAND

***

Now, let me tell you something about the band and what it does. The band basically is an inflatable band around the top of your stomach (think swimming arm bands). When you eat, the food sits just above the band in a much smaller space and makes you feel full on much less food. Two days after my first fill, eating half a banana felt like I'd stuffed a three-course meal.

The amount of fluid in your band will gradually increase until 'optimal.' The way you know what 'optimal' is? if you drink water and spit it back up (a semi-puke) – then your band is too tight.

Since there was no post-op care at the private hospital I went to, or available on the NHS, I had to find a community of 'banders' to answer simple questions like,

'Does this feel right?'
'How much should I have my band filled' or
'What happens when you have a 'stuck' issue?'
I found this community on YouTube.

'Stucks' are really awful. Basically, you have to chew your food three times as much as you normally would (that's at least twenty times) and eat much slower, assessing if you're full, and stopping when you are.

If you don't, extremely serious complications will occur and you will be unable to ingest anything, even water, until the piece of food you *haven't* chewed properly either comes up or goes down. Eventually, permanent damage can ensue, or much worse: the whole area (the 'pouch' above the band) can collapse over on itself and this could prove fatal.

Equally, if you eat too quickly, the same will happen. It starts with feeling like you've got a lump in your throat, only slightly lower. Then your mouth starts watering (like it does right before you're about to puke), depending on the seriousness of the event, you will start spitting foam, and then the proper puking happens.

Only it's not stomach-acid puke, it's basically all the food you chewed and swallowed, with this really gunky saliva that's thicker than spit and really elastic. This will go on until you upchuck the piece of food that got stuck. After that, you generally feel pukey and shaky for hours afterwards. It's not uncommon to also suffer headaches.

My worst 'stuck' episode started when I was at work one day. I'd pre-prepared daily salads including chopped cucumber. There was one thin slice of cucumber that I hadn't chewed up properly as I was eating too quickly. The slice of cucumber therefore took residence as a 'lid' in my pouch. I was spitting foam and gagging for about eight hours from that point.

I was pretty scared, so I phoned the independent nurse who had visited my home for regular fills, and she said to hold on to the top of a door and drink tea as hot as I could manage (not at the same time) to try and work the piece of food through, or out.

Eventually, the piece came out. I was exhausted, felt wretched, and rarely made the same mistake again. In fact, I've never eaten cucumber since. I even photographed the piece that came up. (People Facebook everything these days, don't they?)

After that, as I wasn't in the right frame of mind to begin with, I just kept on 'testing' the band.

Whilst I never recreated cucumber-gate, I aggravated the band so much that I inflamed the area around it, which eventually caused serious episodes of acid reflux at times when I wasn't eating. At one time, it occurred while I was driving (see Acid Reflux), and that was my turning-point: I had to get the band 'de-activated.'

Deactivation means that I had all but 1cc of fluid taken out of my band. I can never have the band removed without other possible serious complications and life-changes.

Seven years on, I still get reminded that I have a gastric band, albeit a deactivated one. I still can't eat big meals; I can't eat anything too quickly, and I *must* chew my food to within an inch of its life.

Last night, I ate two turkey steaks, and I didn't chew them up properly, or eat slowly enough. That was at about eight p.m. I was gagging and puking 'til ten thirty p.m. then I went to bed with a sick bag. I woke up still feeling shaky and 'pukey' at two a.m., went downstairs and drank some water (to purposefully induce puking, to try and dislodge the stuck food). I puked some more at four a.m. My alarm went off for work at five a.m. and I felt queasy, shaky, and generally unwell.

As I was pretty warped psychologically, it was doomed from the start. I was always going to try and 'cheat' the system. My thoughts last night, while puking, were,

'Wow, I wish this was cookie dough ice-cream.'

Turkey escalope with garlic butter and parmesan crumb was not the nicest thing to have to taste twice.

It seems I can even have a sense of humor when I'm putting my health (and career) in jeopardy for my frequent 'howling' at the toilet bowl.

Gimmicks

Points, sins (recently changed to 'syns' to skew the negative term), freebies, days-off, meal replacements.

They exist for 'my' convenience – because the modern human doesn't have time to weigh and measure. We don't have time to count calories. They are all gimmicks, invented so that I don't have to consider what I am putting in. Someone else has done the 'hard' work.

For instance, in the context of meal-replacement-drink diets –

'Just drink this three times a day' is way easier for us to do than,

'Calculate your BMR, eat less than that -in three meals that are nutritionally balanced.'

If I actually broke down all the gimmick diets, I'm sure I'd see that under the hood they are all the same: calorie controlled and (generally) nutritionally balanced, and if I get really deep in this regard, I can blow my own mind: *What else could they be?*

I need to continue to educate myself about calories and nutrition, BMRs and BMIs. I need to continue to learn about the science behind it. I need to get less lazy about nutrition.

Otherwise, what is it I'm learning?

I'm learning how many points are in that snickers bar -not *why* I want it, whether I get any nutritional value from it, or why I might feel guilty afterwards.

H is for

Habits

I've learned more about the mechanics and definition of 'a habit'.

A habit is a learned behavior, basically, one that I perform 'automatically.' It's an electrical pathway in the brain that I have strengthened by doing it over and over again. Getting dressed is a habit, knowing where I live is a habit, brushing my teeth is a habit, riding a bike is a habit, and it follows then that knowing how to have sex is a learned behavior, too (since that's like riding a bike, apparently).

And so is overeating.

More than this, habits are not just things I physically do, but how I think, or feel, can also be a habit.

According to some science journals, it takes an average of 66 days to form a habit – some say 100.

Does it follow, then, that it takes 66 days on average to break one? Not sure about the science of that, since we're all different, and no one really knows the strength of the habit we're trying to break, how long we've had it, how or why we might rely on it.

See also Change One Thing

Hunger

'Noun: A feeling of discomfort or weakness caused by lack of food.'

I've learned about the biological events that happen in our bodies to tell us we're hungry – and they are fascinating – I highly recommend a good read on that subject, if you're interested. I just never imagined that so many things that had to happen for our stomach to rumble.

I think that, as I make a habit of over-eating, I also lose the ability to recognise whether I am actually hungry, or perhaps I never allow myself to get hungry. It's all very complex isn't it.

But isn't it a sign of over-indulgence that I can no longer remember what feeling hungry is like?

I used to work with someone who observed Ramadan. This, although I am no expert, meant not eating while the sun was up, 'to remind oneself about others less fortunate' she told me. There's a lot more to it than that but you know, that's the gist. She would wake up before sunrise for breakfast, and then she wouldn't eat until after sunset.

Something about this really appealed to me on a personal level. To go back to that 'deprived' state, to remember what it feels like to be hungry, and subsequently, to appreciate what we have, and what others don't.

I even considered joining her for Ramadan one year. I didn't (such is my strength of character), but I tried to support her at work in other ways. I still think it's a kind and noble thing to do. What I learned from her is that it takes a huge amount of psychological strength to endure it. The same strength, I would imagine, it would take to break an old, worn-in habit.

Hunger-Scale

So, am I hungry or thirsty? Do I know the difference? Another nifty tool I found during my endless dieting, was to spend some time asking myself if I was hungry or thirsty. This is a form of mindfulness (which just means 'paying attention').

To do this, I would go grab a flashy wine glass, fill it with water and perhaps ice, sit down and enjoy it. After that, I would decide whether it was the water I needed or if I was actually hungry.

There are many levels of hunger which are useful to learn too. This is a scale I currently have on my fridge, though it might be more useful to put it where you prepare food -at eye-level:

- 10 Stuffed to the point of feeling sick
- 9 Very uncomfortably full, need to loosen belt/clothing
- 8 Uncomfortably full, feel stuffed
- 7 Very full, feel as if you have over-eaten
- 6 Comfortably full, satisfied
- 5 Comfortable, neither hungry nor full.
- 4 Beginning signals of hunger
- 3 Hungry, ready to eat
- 2 Very hungry, unable to concentrate
- 1 Starving, dizzy, irritable

As an experiment, I printed this out and put it in front of my auntie when she sat down to eat. She first decided how hungry she was (four), and then, still reading the scale, she actually stopped eating before she might normally have (six).

If you start at four, the amount of food you need to get to five or six is way less than you might think. Try it for myself; it's very interesting. You might even decide you're not hungry at all!

I is for

Incontinence

Being overweight did, for a while, weaken my pelvic floor, because of the weight of fat on the bladder. The more overweight I got, the more I courted the chances of suffering from incontinence.

This limits my ability to sneeze, laugh, and cough without 'oops'ing, and so introduces the world of the 'oops' sanitary products. Just another thing one doesn't talk about.

So, there are about four different sizes of 'oops' products out there.

- **One Drip:** The first are teeny tiny panty liners that save me from the odd drip, which might happen while watching a Trump speech (hilarity) or having to stop suddenly while driving.
- **Two Drips:** This size exists for drips that happen more than once a day, the kind of 'oops' that make me freeze, and say, 'Uh-oh.'
- **Three drips:** These are the ones that make me feel like I'm wearing a rolled-up sweater between my legs, and by this time I need to look into pelvic-floor strengthening exercises and other tools. I might be forced to wear these if I'm suffering from a bad winter cold, or stress.

I've never gotten to the stage of the Pants: These are adult nappies, basically. I'll promote myself to these when I've given up entirely on my pelvic-floor muscles or am post-op from a medical condition that affects my bladder. I wonder if they make these in a size twenty-four. I'm really sorry I can't speak about post-childbirth continence, as I've never had kids, but I do understand that incontinence after childbirth is quite common.

Several years ago, I actually tried one of the tools available for this condition. It was called the 'Noon Aquaflex Cones.' They are still available today and cost about £30. This is a weight-lifting tool for your pelvic floor, and I found it really interesting. To use them, you put one of three different weights inside a small, insertable cone (start with the lowest) and insert it. Then you have to flex the right muscles to keep it in position. Vaginal weightlifting. My pelvic floor would now put Arnold Schwarzenegger to shame if he was a woman.

Since doing this, and by losing weight, I've had no issues with incontinence whatsoever, certainly for the past five years.

The vaginal weightlifting is fun to try. If anything, it's a really useful tool to learn about your pelvic floor muscles, particularly where they *actually* are. I learned that they are not the same muscles you flex when you're holding in a pee. They are further back. Try it out, especially if Pilates is not working for you.

J is for

Jargon

See Gimmicks

Jaw Winking Syndrome

This is an honorable mention. Found this little gem while I was pondering over J's relating to being fat. Nothing immediately sprang to mind, but I found this.

jaw-winking syndrome n.

'An increase in the width of the eyelids that occurs during chewing, sometimes accompanied by a rhythmic raising of the upper lid when the mouth is open and its subsequent drooping when the mouth is closed. Also called Marcus Gunn phenomenon.'

Learn something new every day, I always say. I will eat my next meal in front of the mirror. And I could bet you raised your upper lid while reading that.

Jersey

The fabric, not the place.

For me, jersey is an absolute GOD-send. Jersey, as I'm sure we all know, is a stretchy fabric that's generally soft and very comfortable. Most of my casual, about-the-house clothes are jersey, as are the majority of my 'going outside' clothes. I just can't get enough of it.

I love it because you can get away with going a few sizes down, which means that jersey clothes are generally more available. The black harem pants I'm wearing right at this moment are jersey. And they are two sizes smaller than I'd usually need, from a store I wouldn't normally shop at.

Other stores that stock jersey are fair game too. I can buy work clothes, tops, and tunics from a store in a lesser size because they are jersey. I still must be careful, though; if it's figure-hugging jersey I avoid it (usually because the bra underneath makes my boobs look ridiculous).

I found a jersey top a couple of years ago in a store I shop at (that does not stock my size). It was a black, ¾ sleeve, great length (covered the belly) and on the front had a black and electric blue geometric print. Super smart, very classy. Well, I just about wore that top to work three times a week. Loved it. Felt like a million dollars in it. I still have it somewhere, but it's got a hole in it, so I can't wear it out anymore.

I've heard some people say that overweight people shouldn't wear stretchy fabrics. Wearing a non-stretch fabric helps you know when you are gaining weight. Clothes that are capable of getting 'tight' are a good thing. They are an early signal that the waistline is expanding.

The flip side of that is we try and pull on our non-stretch clothes one day and find that we can't zip them. That can be traumatizing and depressing.

You might suggest that stretchy fabrics hide us from acknowledging that we are overweight.

I already know this. And I'm not sure there's any harm in us being kind to ourselves (by being comfortable) while we figure this thing out, is there?

I am getting much more adventurous with clothing because of the array of fantastic plus-sized clothing ranges that are available. But in terms of comfort and self-confidence, to me, there's no beating jersey.

K is for

Kidnapping

Oh yeah, you betcha. On account of me spending four years or so at a sneaky-beaky Government Agency (No, it's not like 'Spooks'-no deep fat fryers were used).

On induction, we are taught certain things to enhance and maintain our own safety: shredding everything that has your name on it; taking different routes to work; not congregating or socialising in groups; keeping a tightly locked down, minimal internet presence; not acknowledging work colleagues in public near the workplace; and making sure you are not followed or approached by strangers. Afterwards, over lunch, we had a little chat amongst ourselves about all the new things we had to now incorporate into our lives. The conversation developed into the whole kidnapping scenario -at which point I switch off.

'Why, Samantha' I hear you ponder, 'I would think that's an extremely important thing to know about.'

Well, I say to you, my lovely reader: No one is going to bundle this body into the back of a van without a forklift. For now, I will have to live with the fact that I'm not a kidnap-able candidate for the bad guys.

Kindness

Before my last *'that's it, I'm going on a diet'* phase, there was one particular thing that I noticed above anything else – my mood changes (which subsequently had a detrimental effect on how I saw myself).

It's really on a variety of levels and, sure, there are certain other external factors. However, I've noticed that after eating something I probably shouldn't have, I would begin to feel morose. I'd snap at my two poor cats (who I love like kids) and have a downward spiraling negative attitude about everything.

Being fat makes everything more difficult and, post-pizza, my thought would be,

'Okay, now you just intentionally made things even more difficult' or, the more common thought, *'why did you just eat THAT?'*

Aches, pains, skin problems, self-esteem are all affected by what I eat. The more weight my body has to handle, the more my back will ache. The more crap I eat, the more I am likely to get gout (which feels like you've got steel splinters in your ankle joints) or diabetes, headaches, bad posture, chafing, dehydration, incontinence, bad menstrual cycles, constipation (or, the opposite, 'the squirts'). It's all one big chain reaction.

I recently had a small party for a few very close friends at my house. My best friend arrived first, and we were chatting about food (we often do).

'You know what?' I said, 'Eating [crap] makes me thoroughly miserable.'

That tiny statement was an epiphany for me. I suddenly recalled that the first thing I think about when I wake up -the very first question I ask myself every single morning, was - *'What did you eat yesterday?'*

I had literally programmed my brain to do this *every* time I opened my eyes in the morning before I've even lifted my head off the pillow. If I'd been eating rubbish the day before, I'd force myself to remember it, and before I'd even put my feet on the floor, I was punishing myself and calling myself names.

So, not only did I feel awful immediately after eating said crap, but I'd make myself feel bad about it the next day. That was my starting state in the morning, my baseline: to be unkind to myself.

These days I've been practicing being kind to myself. I've accepted the fact that my diet isn't great. My weight is awful. But it isn't getting worse. I'm not gaining weight. I am okay. It's easier said than done, you know. Waking up and saying to myself, *'God, you're amazing'* or *'It's going to be an awesome day'* or even *'You're okay, everything is okay'* takes a lot of thought.

Meditation has helped me do this, with a technique called 'noting.'

Noting is, as it sounds, *noticing* when my thoughts spiral off into something negative, noting it, and then bringing my thoughts back to something else. To *'abort mission and return to base.'* This could be anything - like a deep breath in, visualising my chest rising and falling. That 'return' gives me a chance to consciously choose what to say, in place of,

'You shouldn't have eaten that yesterday, fatty.'

I say it out loud if I have to or look in a mirror and make a silly face.

It takes a lot of practice to notice my thoughts spiraling off into bad territory. But master it I have, and I've learned that noting is one of the most powerful tools I can use.

Try it tomorrow morning. Wake up and pull the most stupid face you can. If you're smiling by the time you stand up, it's far more likely you'll have a positive day. Or at least a better chance at one.

L is for

Lists

I've always found lists to be useful, even ones I recite in my head. I write down what I won't miss about being overweight, and what I might look forward to when I am are maintaining a healthy weight. I read it often. My list is as long as a can of silly string, but here's a small example:

1. I look forward to fitting into bathtubs (and not creating a vacuum that can bend metal).
2. I look forward to being able to wear knee-high boots (rawr!).
3. I look forward to wearing a bra that doesn't double as a grocery bag.
4. I won't miss people on trains using your hip as an armrest. I won't miss sweaty summers.
5. I won't miss not having any energy.
6. I won't miss taking the lift one floor. I look forward to sexy curves.
7. I look forward to feeling like myself again.

Lighter Life (Review)

Lighter Life is a meal replacement diet. Three drinks a day, milkshakes or soup, and a granola-type bar, all of which are provided for a fixed weekly fee.

Whilst I've been on this briefly, (14 pounds lost), I thought I'd feature my best friend here, as she had a terrifying experience after reaching her goal on this diet. So, I interviewed her, and here's what she told me.

Q. How much did you lose on Lighter Life?

A. Ten stone and two pounds, altogether, over eight and a half months. [64.4kg]

Q. Why did you decide on Lighter Life as an option?

A. Well, it was my old boss who made me do it; she was sick of hearing me moan about losing weight. She was overweight herself and had read about it, so she took me along to a Lighter Life class meeting and said, 'I think you should try this.' – I'd never considered it before. She wasn't being mean; she was trying to help. I remember feeling it was a good idea.

Q. What were your first couple of days like?

A. I signed up straight away, and there was a group starting the following week. Honestly, I just fell straight into it. I remember on the first day, I was cutting up grapes for the girls' lunch boxes and I went to eat one, and thought, Oooh, no, can't do that anymore. To me, doing it was the easy part.

Q. Did you have 'bad' days or weeks?

A. I signed up for a hundred days to start with, and I remember looking at my calendar and thinking only ninety-nine more days left. Although, I knew it would take longer than that. I never had bad days at all; I never deviated once. Anyone who knows me knows that I am crap when it comes to things like that. I almost felt like I'd been...drugged! Who was I? and what have they done with the real me?

I tell you what it was, it was the fact that you literally cannot eat anything, other than what was on the plan. I never remember feeling hungry; I mean, I went through Christmas day without food! Had my soup. Black coffee with sweetener and diet coke were my best friends. It was a control thing, I think. On normal diets, you still have to eat, and you still have to choose. And the consistent four-or five-pounds loss every week–that was a big 'pull.'

Q. So that was what kept you going? The big weight loss?

A. Well, yeah. I just wanted to get to the end.

Q. Was there a time when you wondered what you were going to do when it finished [the plan]?

A. Oh yeah, that frightened me. Eating [normal food] for the first time frightened me. At the end, you do 'maintenance' for about three months. During this time, you gradually re-introduce food. It was scary.

Q. So, how was your weight when you were on maintenance?

A. My weight was stable, I mean, I was not gaining weight at all. I probably maintained for about three or four months afterwards.

Q. While you were on the plan, did you worry at all about your health?

A. No, I went to the Doctor every twenty-eight days for my blood pressure to be checked. I think psychologically, that 'ticked' the box for me.

Q. How soon afterwards did you become ill?

A. I started having 'tummy' problems, quite soon after I started eating again. I'd get these chronic pains in my upper abdomen. There was no rhyme or reason to it – no particular food that set off the pain.

The Doctors did blood tests and whatnot, and at first, nothing. They couldn't find anything wrong. Looking back, I think it was my body not being able to cope with fat again, which is why I have gall stones.

I'd been in a constant state of ketosis for so long, over eight months. So, there was all this bile in my gall bladder that had solidified, which is where the stones come from.

At first, no one actually said that it was because of the diet I'd been on. Then, I was going to visit my Husband in Germany, but I had a bad stomach again, so I submitted to more blood tests before I left.

When I got home, I had a note on my doorstep from the Doctor's office, saying that I had to contact them, urgently. When I got there my Doctor said, 'I haven't got very good news, but you're very seriously ill and we don't know what it is' Up to then I thought I had stomach problems, but it was all to do with my liver. I knew things were bad then because while I was there my doctor called the consultant surgeon at the hospital and got me an appointment that very afternoon. When I got there, the Consultant told me that my liver function was showing a score of something like 1,970 and a normal person should be about 60.

'You should be either an alcoholic, or dead. But you're obviously neither.'

He went on to say that he suspected some kind of Hepatitis. But again, they never found anything decisive.

Finally, he concluded that it was to do with the diet I'd been on. He said he couldn't prove it scientifically, but that he could categorically say that those very low-calorie meal 'replacements' screw your body up.

Q. What would your advice be to others considering a meal-replacement diet?

A. Just don't do it. You'll put the weight back on, you won't learn anything, and it messes with your insides. You know, you need a balanced diet, not just 'calories. Christ, you'd have to be blind, deaf, and dumb not to know how a good diet can help you lose weight.

I think very low calories diets have their place, for people who have some control. But most of the people who are getting to this point are not in control. I do think the industry preys on people like me. The industry is improving, though. Weightwatchers, for instance, is moving towards the whole 'wellbeing' thing, and it's a good way to go.'

M is for

Massage

See Beauticians

Metabolism

See BMR

Men

-and their attitude towards dieting.

I do not intend to incur the wrath of the internet by generalizing here, but these are what I've picked up from the men around me.

What I find interesting is how differently men view food and dieting (in my experience). I happened to be chatting to a colleague at work recently about diets, and one thing he said stuck with me.

I was explaining that I hadn't eaten a meal the night before, as I had visitors 'round and they left late, so I didn't bother. I hadn't had breakfast the morning after either, and so I was clock-watching for lunch that day.

I added that since my bestie and I had gone to a spa (and had a count-free day) the week or so before, I wanted a really good weight loss this week.

'I don't understand you women and your diets' he said.

I think what he was getting at, was that men 'see' food differently than women. In his world, a meal is something you just do, in order for your body to function. With women, weight seems to be a big deal and we tend to have more of an emotional attachment to food and weight.

In fact, the only emotional attachment I've ever known a man put to food, is a soldier and his kebab at the end of a boozy evening, or pie at a football match.

So, how is it that women learn to attach emotions to food more than men do? Have we ever heard guys say, 'I deserve that' or 'I'll start again tomorrow'? If they want something, they have it. Now, whether they are better at hiding any emotional attachment they might have, is another matter.

I believe it also depends upon the generation that you are talking to. To my father, for instance, things are very black and white. He was brought up during the War. Rations and 'growing-your-own' taught you that you eat what's put in front of you, and that you're lucky to get that.

So, he just doesn't understand that these days there's 'too much to eat.' He doesn't understand how to get to be overweight nor does he 'get' the whole emotional eating thing.

His solution: 'Well, if you want to lose weight, just stop eating.' It's that simple to him. I totally respect that; I totally get it.

Of course, there are some modern-day 'diets' that do appeal to men, because they are 'manly' and masculine; I'm referring to 'The Caveman' type diets – eat only what you can kill or grow myself, but I'm not sure than men have the same motivation as women. I think men embark on these types of diets more for health reasons, whereas, I would venture to say that for women, it's perhaps more aesthetics first.

According to the World Health Organization, there are more women who are overweight than men.

I don't think breaking the emotional attachment with food is the answer either. Because that means that I wouldn't apply the same logic to healthy food. Food should be a joy; it shouldn't be shovelled down, nor should it have a negative effect on me after I've eaten it.

I think half the battle here is finding healthy food that I actually like, and learning not only to look forward to it, but to feel great after eating it.

See also Preparation

Mindfulness

I love seeing all the new 'buzz-words' popping up and becoming viral on the internet. This one's no exception.

I've learned that mindfulness just means 'paying attention' or, more specifically, 'paying attention to the present moment.'

I was recently chatting to a weightlifter (quite a 'fit' one, if you know what I mean, wink) and he was 'selling' a concept that was, basically, mindfulness. Only instead of concentrating on your breath, he was visualising his muscles fibres as he lifted weights.

I drew from that, that I can quite literally apply the concept of Mindfulness to anything. Mindful tooth-brushing, for instance. I think it's great, and mastering it is a key to unlocking how to control my unconscious habits (like buying a snickers bar in the petrol station).

Anyway, back to the point. Mindful eating means paying attention to what I'm eating. How it looks, what its texture feels like, what it smells like. Take a few seconds on each while I'm eating.

What this also does, is slow down my eating. Which is also good. Humans are supposed to chew. Chewing prepares the food for other things that happen once I've swallowed. The more I can chew, the better. Chewing and slowing down also give me time to recognise when I'm full.

See also Hunger

Mood Swings

See Kindness

Mirrors

A few years ago, I had a friend stay over and we were getting ready to go out.

'Do you have a mirror?' she asked, as she took the towel off her head.

'Nope. No mirrors here.' She stopped in her tracks.

'What? None?'

She had that look on her face, as if she just realised I was a serial killer.

Thinking back to those days, I did almost definitely have something wrong with my head.

I went through a phase of cutting the tickets out of every piece of clothing I owned. One of the reasons for that was, I told myself, that I'd once seen a relative inspecting the ticket on something of mine.

In reality, I think it was because I didn't want to be reminded how overweight I was every time I got dressed in the morning.

I should mention that I didn't go around my house and remove all the mirrors, I just didn't have any.

Perhaps that's another subconscious thought -not reminding myself of my current state.

These days, practicing self-kindness, and meditation, has definitely 'chilled me out' in that regard.

I have mirrors now. Well, 'head and shoulder' ones, and I am considering buying a full-length mirror.

I think it would be good to stand in front of a full-length mirror and re-connect with parts of my body I haven't seen for years. Literally years. How sad is that.

It's all me, after all. And day by day I'm learning that I love me.

So, when I can, I'm going to buy a full-length mirror, stand in front of it, and have an out-loud conversation with my parts.

I have an overwhelming desire to thank all the parts of my body for all the shit I've put it through and renew the relationship I have with it.

And maybe I'll have a good cry. Yes, I'll do that.

N is for

Necessity

I've been pondering. The difference between over or unhealthy eating, and other addictions, is that I *need* food to *literally* survive.

It's not something I can drop and walk away from entirely, like alcohol, cigarettes, or narcotics.

Food is a necessity. Re-programming these habits, therefore, is more difficult, isn't it?

Not least because I tend to be constantly bombarded with food in my daily life, and have a deep-ingrained set of social beliefs where food is concerned:

Cakes on birthdays; toffee-apples on Bonfire-night; chocolate eggs at Easter; turkey feast at Christmas.

Not only do I have to work on re-programming my habits, but I have to learn to cope with those social situations where *not* participating might not be an option.

See also Preparation

Needles

See Gastric Band

Negativity

See Kindness

Noting

See Kindness

Nutrition

Nutrition refers to the 'provision of essential nutrients necessary to support human life and health.'

I won't go too deeply into this because I think that as I become more mindful about the whole weight loss experience, I will naturally learn the nutritional composition of food. What I will say, is that if I follow gimmick diets, I will never educate myself sufficiently to understand what I'm putting in.

If I'm given a 'points allowance' every day, then I'm just going to concentrate on how many points I can have, how many points I've eaten, how many points I have left, and the points value of things.

I'm not learning what's 'under the hood.' Whilst gimmicks might be useful in busy lives for a while, I believe I need to learn about nutrition as I go along.

A snickers bar might have 12 points, which might be within my allowance, but what are those 12 points made of, do I know?

Granted, I think 'points and other gimmicks would perhaps teach me to choose wisely, but I'm not sure this alone is entirely the answer.

O IS FOR

Obesity

Obesity means the accumulation of excess body fat, to the extent that it may have a detrimental effect on health.

This is an intensely complicated but interesting subject. It's a global epidemic, and this is not the book for that analysis. I'd just be re-writing what has already been written.

So, should I be concerned about this epidemic as an individual?

One of the teachings of mindfulness has taught me is that I release cortisol and adrenalin when I am reading or stressing about things I can do nothing about. Therefore, if we keep doing this, I am literally poisoning my brain.

If I am constantly stewing over the fact that I am part of some global epidemic, it's not going to do a great amount for my self-esteem, either.

The best I can do is be concerned (and mindful) with myself as an individual. My success at this, could mean that I eventually educate my kids and future parents, and if this happens it could make a difference.

Sheesh. That was a bit grandiose, wasn't it?

P is for

Panic Attacks

See Anxiety

Plateaus

Many a time, at the many slimming classes I've attended, I've seen individuals who won't lose weight, or they lose half a pound (which they really just pee'd out before they got to class). Or they put on a pound.

'I just don't get it, I've been really good this week,' I hear them telling the class leader.

Heard that before? Yeah, me too.

In every likelihood, they hopped off the wagon that week, had an event they hadn't planned for, or got dragged along to some work social.

For me, if I've had successful weight loss and that weight loss has slowed or stopped, I should consider increasing exercise. Recalculating my BMR regularly will refresh my daily calorie requirement. Also, if I've lost that weight, I need to exercise for longer to burn the same amount. So, it's likely that which is causing the plateau.

Or I might just be bored out of my mind with the food I'm eating, despite any success.

Certain prescription drugs can also cause a slow-down in weight loss.

One of the reasons I no longer go to weigh-in class events is because, once, my mum hit a plateau while she was being treated for a brain tumor.

We'd go to slimming classes because it was something we had in common: we were always dieting. I think Mum used to do it for me, really. I never ever saw her as 'fat' and she was always super active, always on the go. I think it was her way of encouraging me, and also something we could do together. I miss that.

On one particular occasion, the class leader delivered the news that Mum hadn't lost any weight that week.

Mum explained that she was taking prescription medication. She as too dignified to tell her what for. (I always loved that about Mum).

And I swear to GOD, the class leader rolled her eyes as if to say she'd heard all the excuses before.

I almost burst into tears on behalf of my mum; I was so angry. On this occasion, she had other things to worry about, you know -surviving, and the class leader was rolling her eyes that she hadn't lost a pound that week.

Mum died not long after. And I never set foot in any slimming class again.

Preparation

Since, I've dieted for most of my life, there has definitely been occasion where I've said to myself,

'That's it! I'm starting [the diet] tomorrow!'

When I did, I almost definitely failed shortly afterwards.

Even if I joined a slimming class as a brand-new member, the class expected me to start as soon as I got home, and I could guarantee that that was the night I finished of the rest of the cheesecake that was in the fridge.

That sure ain't preparation.

I've learned that, if I decide to embark upon a life-changing journey, the very key to success is preparation. This gives me much more of a chance to succeed.

So, I made a list that seems to work. I allow myself five days to complete this preparation. This list is roughly in order:

- **Visit the doctor**

Tell them I am planning to lose weight and ask them for any advice specific to my health. They will probably weigh me, so that will give me a little extra 'reinforced-accountability.' They might even recommend a nutritionist if I am deficient in a certain nutrient or allergic to certain foods. We don't know everything about ourselves, and the doctor might even tell me something I didn't know.

- **Tell. Everyone.**

Secondly, I tell everyone I know that I am re-programming my nutritional intake, detoxing, changing my eating habits; I tell them anything other than 'I'm going on a diet.'

If I'm going 'on' something, that indicates that there's some kind of 'end-date.' This is a permanent change that I am committing to, not just something I'm doing to get to some kind of goal.

Most importantly, this gives me nowhere to 'hide.' If I haven't told my best friend, the chances are I'll use them as an enabler. I can pop 'round there for lattes and donuts without any problems. They will be my little 'fat cave.'

Gosh, I just realised what I did there.

To the fat cave, fat Sam!

- **Research and Plan Groceries**

I research the eating plan that I'm going to be embarking upon. If I'm joining a slimming 'club' (doubt it unless its an online version) then I visit their website, sign up, and look at the recipes.

I write a list of everything I'm going to need for at least the first week. Most online grocery stores have a feature where I can paste in a list and name it, so I do that.

I make sure that if I'm going to order groceries online, I'm not going to be wandering off down the virtual cake aisle looking for low-fat something-or-other. For the time being, this is not part of my life anymore.

- **Learn my list and stick to it.**

Whilst on the site, I remove from favourites everything that might tempt me or that I've bought before, if it isn't part of the plan, and make sure that nothing gets offered to me at checkout that isn't on my list.

- **Choose meals for ME**

Once I've decided upon the plan I'm going to follow, I examine it carefully for anything that might put me off-course.

For instance, if I despise cabbage soup and the plan has me eating that in one of the dinner courses on a Friday night, I'm going to start dreading it.

Once I start dreading it, I'm going to try to avoid it. Once I avoid it, I'm leaving myself open to replacing it with something that's not on my plan.

One book I recently bought (see Blood Sugar Diet) had breakfast, lunch, dinner, and snacks all planned out for me, for eight weeks.

Aside from being a bit presumptuous (and godly expensive), I had no appetite for a lot of the stuff, so instead I picked what appealed to me.

I examine my list for variety and alternatives. If for some reason I can't get cucumber from the store that week, what will I do?

Also, I make sure the meals and recipes are ones I've either done before or are within my capabilities. I pick the meals I imagine myself most confident at preparing.

If I find I'm only confident with a small number of the meals, then I have to consider whether I can cope with the same meals for a week. Consider whether it's the right plan for me, and if not, start prep again.

- **Plan for Events**

I recount a typical week in my head. Check my calendar: Do I have something I do regularly? Lunch with the ladies? Friday night cocktails? Take-out Tuesdays? I consider this and decide now what I'm going to do.

I plan for it, and then tell everyone who's involved. If I visit a particular restaurant every week with the girlies, I decide now what I'm going to choose. I examine it, count it, plan it, and tell everyone.

- **Calculate my BMR, monthly**

I calculate my Base Metabolic Rate, whichever plan I've chosen—even one that doesn't need me to count (see Gimmicks). The BMR tells me how many calories my body needs per day. (see Base Metabolic Rate)

I plan to do this every month, as it will change. I put a recurring reminder in my calendars, tell Cortana, Alexa, or whoever else runs my 'i-Life'. I've got a nifty little widget that works in MS Excel. Otherwise, there are a ton of calculators on the internet.

- **Calculate my BMI monthly**

Calculate my Body Mass Index. This will tell me how much extra fat you are carrying, and therefore how much I need to lose.

- **Prepare and Practice my App/Diary**

I sit down for an hour and make sure my diary -whatever that might be, is ready to go. If this means practicing using it, adding meals, adding recipes, then I do that. I could be using it for well over a year, so I have to be comfortable with it. If during this session I decide that it isn't for me, I've got time to change it.

- **Record Groceries in App**

I record everything that comes through my door in terms of food. I order groceries online and scan the barcode as I'm unpacking the stuff and putting it away. (This would work just as well if I scanned the barcode every time I dropped something in my shopping cart while at the store).

This means that everything that I could potentially eat or drink is listed in my app, ready for me to 'tick box' it in my food diary.

There are other barcode reader apps, but the one at MyFitnessPal is by far the best; their reader is not so 'buggy' as others.

- **Clear the fridge -Do NOT have a 'Night Before the Diet' meal.**

I've done this before, and immediately regretted it. That last bit of cheesecake, the lasagna from yesterday, the choc ice that I forgot was in the freezer. I get rid of it.

I remember the day before starting 'Lighter Life' I had a great big bowl of tuna-mayo pasta. Aside from being extraordinarily unhealthy, it does nothing to reinforce your psychological resolve to change.

I practice meditating instead or spend a couple of hours making space in my wardrobe. I drink some chamomile tea and have an early night. I read or add to the list I've made about all the things I'm looking forward to.

Q is for

Quick Fixes

Nothing to see here (there are none).
   See Diets, Gimmicks

R is for

Realism

Be Realistic.

Most women are NOT a size 10. There is a reason when the sales come around all the 8's and 10's are the only ones left on the rail. Think about that.

And while most men (sorry chaps, generalizing), fantasize about size-4 supermodels (would they know what to do with one, I wonder?). According to most men surveyed, they actually prefer voluptuous, luxurious figures - something to hold, or grab - whatever floats your boat.

Girls, if you're with a chap who wants you at 5% body fat (which is what one boyfriend said to me once, I kid you not) then either re-educate him or kick him to the curb.

When you are happy with the way you look, keep that look. And keep it for you.

Reasons (and Excuses)

See Plateaus

Rosacea

At the time I was diagnosed with Rosacea, no one knew what caused it. However, having experienced it for several years I have personally learned that there are several factors involved.

First of all, I'll explain my version of rosacea. When it began it started on my forehead and spread to my nose and cheeks.

Some refer to it as 'adult acne'; however, that's not how it presented itself to me.

To anyone who hasn't experienced what rosacea feels like, imagine your forehead having a bad sunburn, and then dousing it with vinegar.

It stings, somewhat.

Over the years of suffering it, I definitely concluded that stress and a bad diet plays a large part in attacks.

Being overweight tends to aggravate stress and anxiety, so rosacea is just another condition that is aggravated by weight problems.

Since then, I've gone through menopause and my Rosacea is gone. Just vanished. And I can't remember the last time I had an attack.

I still have enlarged pores on areas of my skin where the rosacea was, and significant redness; however, it's nothing that a good moisturizer can't treat.

If you suspect you might have Rosacea, see your doctor. Depending on its severity, they might start you off on a topical gel. I found that made it worse, (and peeled off during the day making me look like my face had started falling off), and so I was put on antibiotics.

If you do have it, then I feel for you, babe, truly. Know that, in my experience, it's temporary. Do your own research and, as I'm sure I've said before, do what works for you.

Rubbing

Chafing; see Uniform, Femininity

S is for

Self Esteem

'I am worth knowing.'

This was the epiphany for me when I was researching my way through some pretty bleak self-esteem issues. Self-esteem could be described as how I might see myself: my evaluation of my own worth.

Overweight or not, external and internal events can have a detrimental effect on my self-esteem. At one point, I felt that I was so fat that I didn't deserve to be 'part of the world' and just walking amongst people made me feel chronically ashamed of my appearance. I got over that with a lot of therapy.

Let me relay to you an intensely personal piece of work that I did during the time I was in that therapy. I was asked to write things down that defined who I was and to do it quickly without thinking too much about it.

I did it, to such great affect that it moved my therapist to tears because the parts of my personality displayed by what I'd written were hidden by my lack of self-worth:

'My name is Samantha; I like wearing black. I'm always on a diet. I like swimming. I ate glass things when I was a kid. I did a Ouija in my boss's office once. I publish vampire stories. I've had my drink spiked. I run a website. I get a weird ache in the pit of my stomach when I think of the sea. I like heavy metal. When I was four, I loved a mohair scarf

that I was inseparable from. I like red lip-gloss. I've seen and had a conversation with death. I like VAST. I like unravelling old, tangled necklaces. I like tattoos. I like teaching people things I know about. I can ride a quad bike. I've smoked cannabis. I like to sleep. I like picnics. I like men's shoulders. I drive too fast. I like flowers that see fit to grow on the side of a busy road. I like New Orleans. I like reading books. I like silver. I was pregnant once. I like shocking pink and electric blue. I've had sex in the strangest places. I like jade. I like Absolut vodka. I like throwing my summer party. I like breaking software. I like last minute camping trips. I like snow. I like sea horses and scuba diving. I died once. I used to eat daisies. I can ride horses. When I was eight, I got an Iron Maiden single for my birthday. One day I pulled the tail off my pet gerbil by accident. I like waking up with someone. I like the first chill of autumn. I've taken coke. I like purple. I've seen a ghost. I like the smell of wet stone after it's rained. I've only ever worn a bikini once. I like the feeling you get when you lay in a field in the middle of the night and stare up at the stars. I once had my hand pierced. I stabbed myself in the back on a tree swing when I was eight. I taught myself to read music. I like sausage-dogs. I dream about killer whales for reasons known only to my subconscious. I'd go back to sucking my thumb, but it's never the same as when you were four.'

Sizes

See Clothing Sizes

Skirts

I don't wear a skirt very often because my legs rub together until they bleed, usually.

Though as I understand it, you can buy 'comfort' shorts to alleviate this. I never have. Clothes, for me, have to feel natural and comfortable; I do not like feeling 'trussed up' like a turkey.

The only other temporary solution for this is to use some talcum powder and apply on the parts that rub as regularly as I can. I find this is the most comfortable way to wear a skirt if I have to.

That feminine silhouette tends to fade the bigger you get (you get that folding chub of fat behind your knees and you lose the line of your ankles. I wear trousers to hide this.

OK, it doesn't hide the fact that I'm hugely overweight, but it means that, in my mind, someone will look at me and say to themselves,

'Wow, she's BIG,' rather than,

'Wow, she's BIG, look at her legs, and those ankles.'

Society might tell me I've got a chip on my shoulder about this, but I know it to be true. That's entirely my problem, not anyone else's.

Slimfast 1-2-3 Plan (Review)

Pros: Convenient if you're on the move or busy. Quite easy to buy for the week. Lots of snacks. A six-hundred calorie evening meal is generous.

Cons: Eating 6 times a day. Also, it doesn't teach you about nutrition. Not for anyone with a large amount of weight to lose.

I've always been a fan of Slimfast meal-replacement drinks since I get up at 4 a. m. for work. At that time in the morning I can barely walk, much less knock up some scrambled eggs or avocado on toast. I grab one, and drink it at my desk at 6 a. m.

The only trouble seems to be that, in between leaving my house and arriving at my desk, I'll swing by a petrol station and pick a chocolate bar and a massive latte with hazelnut syrup.

The Slimfast website is jam packed full of information and support, recipes, and discussion boards.

The first discussion thread I came across was from someone who had obviously returned from her summer vacation saying '...I was doing so well. . . and the odd over-indulgence became more and more. . . and now I am at the heaviest I have ever been. . . I have no excuses.'

And then the responses saying, 'Never mind, you can do it!' –

Personally, I say avoid these communities at all costs until you are confident with what you are doing myself. It sounds quite harsh, but you have to train your own mind before you can listen to other people who are struggling. However, the Slimfast magazine is super. There was a particularly good article there about the best time of day to exercise which opened with a quote:

'I have to exercise in the morning before my brain figures out what I'm doing.' ~Marsha Doble.

(I've since learned there's actual science showing the effectiveness of this to be true).

The 3-2-1 plan was amazingly easy to buy for. Three snacks, two shakes and one 600-calorie meal. I've taken a liberty here that, perhaps I shouldn't have. I've chosen three-courses for my evening meal: soup, meal, and a dessert – the Slimfast site did not direct me to do this. I did, however, very carefully calculate the calories which amounted to 606 for what I had chosen.

Since I'm a god-awful cook and lazy to boot at the moment, I chose foods for my evening meal from the Sainsbury's 'Be Good to Myself' range. If you can cook, then you can probably drive down the cost of the grocery-haul, as I've chosen 'ready' meals for my evening meal – and these are notoriously more expensive than preparing and cooking the food, myself.

* * *

WEEKLY SHOPPING LIST:

- 4 x Slimfast Ready to Drink Vanilla 325ml £6. 32 3 x Slimfast Ready to Drink Banana 325ml £4. 77
- 2 x 4pk Slimfast Meal Bars, Summer Berry 4x60g £9. 98.
- 7 x Sainsbury's Mushroom & Bacon Tagliatelle, 'Be Good to Myself' 400g £14. 00
- 2 x 5pk McVitie's Galaxy Caramel Cake Bars x5 £2. 50 4 x Cans Sainsbury's Root Vegetable Soup, Be Good to
- Myself 400g £2. 24
- 21 x Slim-fast Chocolate Caramel Snack Bar 26g £11. 13

TROLLEY COST: £54. 89

* * *

I have a fair few Slimfast shakes in the fridge anyway, as they are convenient for me and my lifestyle at the moment. I had a disastrously bad start on this. I wasn't fully prepared psychologically or practically -and was so busy at work in the first few days, I felt like I couldn't face changing my eating habits.

The only casualty of this was me, of course. I continued with my latte and chocolate bar on the way to work. And on some days, I did a late shift while completely un-prepared, and so ended up visiting the vending machine at work a few times during the evening. I also really have no excuse for that packet of crisps on the way home at midnight. And I still ate when I got home. I also made a bad choice with the ready meals; they contained pasta, so made me as sick as a dog on several occasions (see Gastric Band).

I'm not sure the 'eating six times a day' was for me either (shake, snack, meal-bar, snack, dinner, and snack).

In general, for me, this was a complete train wreck.

In hindsight, I should have been better prepared for this, mentally. I hadn't prepared to break the habits I'd formed (like the comfort treats at 5 a. m. on the way to work).

I'd imagine this might work for those who maybe have half a pound to lose before their bikini holiday.

This is really not for anyone who has over fifty pounds to lose *and* has a deep-seated and unhealthy attitude towards food.

Snoring

There are many and various 'snoring aids' on the market. Basically, if you're fat and sleep on your back, you probably snore. One of my old girlfriends used to invite me over to a 'girly night in' – which was a kind of grown-up sleep-over and she'd always say, 'Please don't snore tonight.'

Well, not much you can say to that is there. So, in my overnight bag I'd anxiously pack nasal spray, snore tabs, and sometimes an extra pillow. She'd basically wake me up every time I started to make a noise, shouting from the next room,

'SNORING!'

I'd lie awake eventually, praying for the morning so I could just leave.

So, the girly sleepover always turned into a 'girly no sleep.' She turned out to be a raving psychopath anyway (that's a whole other book), and so that problem quickly went away.

Socks

I know, right!

How did I find a few hundred words to write about fatness and SOCKS? But bear with me, patient reader, with everything else we put ourselves through being fat, you've got to hear me out here.

I was sitting on the train in to work the other day with, you know, the fatness and silently considering my outward state.

Super expensive accessories, pro hairdo. The elasticated black suit-trousers that were a tad too long, the unusually fashionable and very 'now' sweater from 'Phase Eight' because their size eighteens are that generous (thanks, Phase Eight), a new bra that was cutting me a new boob (one day I'll get the size right), some old-lady shoes with extra padding -on account of my bad left heel that gave out on account of all the fatness, and I was thinking, Okay. I look okay. I feel okay, this is my 'base state; this is as happy and as comfortable as I'm ever going to be. I'm all ready to go flounce through my day!

And then, my goddamn knee-high started rolling down my leg.

The bastard! I mean, with everything else going on, just one more thing has got to stick it to me.

My 'old-lady' shoes have an elastic bar diagonally across the front – so I couldn't wear socks (else I'd come off as German Tourist), and I couldn't wear nothing on my feet, since the memory-foam soles inside my 'old-lady' shoes would crumple up into the front and make my dodgy toenail sore.

So, this morning, it was the fifteen-denier knee-highs. Now these bastards come in two sizes. 'Roll-Down-Yer-Leg' or 'Cut-Yer-Leg-Off-At-the-Knee' and, you know, depending on what kind of mood I'm in -I'll pick one or the other.

However, this morning, I think I've picked one of each. The other one is staying up in a way that says, Oh, yeah bitch, I'll stay up here alright, you just wait.

I might pick those kinds when I'm in a particular rant mood because I ate too many calories the night before and I deserve to suffer.

I digress.

So, this thing has started to roll down (because I blinked, probably) and my train's stopping at its destination.

Now, with all these people around, do I just chuckle out loud and say, 'Gosh darn these things' giggle-giggle, and hike up the trouser leg and yank it back up again?

Or do I risk having a 'Nora Batty' and just hope no one notices?

I decide for the latter and just hope the roll doesn't continue down my foot, so it ends up looking like I've got one foot dressed and the other one not. (Like I'd care -I once got in a lift with the Boss's Boss's Boss, whilst wearing a cardigan inside out, tags flapping in the wind. Of course, he was too gracious to mention it).

On following day, I decided to go all-out, and wear fishnet knee-highs. Oh yeah, super-vamp me baby. I'm all about the vampness.

Except, have you ever seen Alien vs Predator, specifically when the guy gets shot at with a net that tightens on his face and, well, doesn't stop? That's what fishnets do to your feet if you're on the heavy side.

I instantly regretted my decision to wear those fishnet jobbies, on a day where I'm traipsing round London all day. My feet ended up looking like pieces of cubist-modern art with blisters. The Tate Modern was all over me about it.

So, day three (yes, this was literally one day after the other) I give in and do the German-tourist thing and wear socks.

Not just any socks, oh no. Posh, slightly thicker, furry-soled, super-smart socks that I remembered do stay in place and do not attempt to cut my feet off at the ankle.

I'm feeling very smug when I step onto the train for my daily commute at 6 a. m. Until I look down and see that I've got one on inside-out and my right foot looks like a yeti wearing and orthopedic sandal.

On day four I give up and wear boots.

Spas (Health/Beauty Spas)

See Beauticians

The Special-K Plan (Review)

Note: This diet no longer exists in the form reviewed.

Having researched this one beforehand, I was dreading planning for this. Based on the shopping list they (very kindly) provide – I don't think I've ever seen so much food in all my life – it appeared that I was either going to be planning a meal, preparing a meal, or eating a meal for two weeks straight.

The shopping list for the week was truly astounding. Was extremely interested to find out just how healthy and vibrant I would feel after two weeks on this one, that's for sure.

As with most 'promotional' diets – this one will not allow you to register if your BMI is over 40. They're scared to tackle the REAL issues, you see:

'As you have a BMI of over 40, we recommend that you contact your GP or health adviser for slimming advice and support.'

So, for the sake of the review, I inserted my starting weight as 203 pounds. A complete lie. I wish it weren't.

'Additionally, if you are pregnant, breastfeeding, diabetic, or have an eating disorder'

– they refer you also. They also ask you for a goal weight, and a date when you can reasonably expect to achieve it. If you set this too low, you will get a message:

'We don't recommend that you lose more than 10% of your body weight, your minimum recommended weight is therefore 13st 1 lbs..' (Typo straight from the web site. Spell-check people, spell-check!)

THE SPECIAL-K PLAN (REVIEW)

On the 14th of July 2011, the estimated goal date calculated was Sept 21, 2011. 20lbs in 69 days. 2lbs a week. Okay, that's reasonable. I was also offered a 'Kick Start Plan' for the first 15 days. Included with this are 'daily emails' and 'motivational hints' to get going. To complete registration and get my plan, I was then asked to answer some questions about myself.

*　*　*

WEEKLY SHOPPING LIST:

What's useful about this plan is that it calculates your weekly shopping list for you, based on your plan.

You can then have that list sent to Tesco, emailed to an email address of your choice, or you can print it.

I tried the 'Tesco' thing. Assuming you have a login – it puts everything you need in your basket.

'Nifty!' you would think.

However, half-way through my endless 'adding to basket', the Special-K website crashed.

'Sorry – we're currently experiencing server issues. We're aware of the issue and hope to be back up and running as soon as possible. Thanks for your patience!'

When I hit the *'Back'* button - my basket was empty. Luckily, a click on *'View full basket'* seemed to show that the goods were retained.

An hour or so and many *'sorry'* error-messages later, I'm about halfway through adding my items to basket. I get to *'Peppered Mackerel'* and it crashed again.

'Oh, SOD it.'

Slow, slow, slow.

Based on a partial shopping list provided, and approximately £80 of food and ingredients, I gave up.

*　*　*

This was a non-starter. Based on the shopping list, which was possibly the biggest shopping list I've ever seen in my life, this was a no-go. I would be doing nothing but preparing meals all day or eating them. I have a life, you know. Pros: Website shopping list clever idea but,

Cons: The website was broken and slow. Unless you are Nigella What's-Her-Face, do not bother.

Extortionately expensive and expansive list of foods. Only for those with nothing else to do in the day *but* prepare meals.

Summer

See Temperature

T is for

Tables

See Fat-shaming

Talcum Powder

Is an absolute 'godsend' for the voluminally-challenged (new phrase, I invented it).

When fat, I feel I lose a certain sense of femininity. (*see Femininity*).

Overall shape distorts, skin changes, I sweat more, things rub together that shouldn't. It's very much a vicious circle. With me, it's,

> 'You're fat, you cover up, you sweat, you feel worse, you eat.' *Ad infinitum.*

I think one of the answers is that whatever I decide to do -be it lose weight, stay as I am, or get bigger (please don't, Sam), it's really important not to lose (or to hang onto every shred of) that sense of being a woman. There needs to be a sense of comfort in my body.

This all seems rather deep for a paragraph on talc, doesn't it! What I'm trying to say is that if there's any step I can take just to feel a bit more comfortable and, perhaps, a bit more feminine, I use it. I put it under my boobs and anywhere the skin creases or rubs and shouldn't. At least it'll make me feel simply better.

If I can find one, I take a compact talc with me to work, so I can freshen up at lunchtime in the summer. Feeling comfortable helps with confidence. Ooh, and I use it at night before I go to sleep, so I won't wake up all sweaty and uncomfortable.

Temperature

Well, it's official. I'm definitely a winter person.

There's nothing better than waking up when it's snowed the night before, or that day at the end of the summer when the air has that first noticeable autumn nip.

Well, that's great. But one of the many reasons that I resolve to lose weight, is that it's usually related to that dreaded feeling of going through another summer, fat.

I'd have to have the hide of a rhino to be unaffected by the temperatures of summer. It's hideous; it's uncomfortable. Skin rubs skin until it bleeds, I'm out of breath quicker, I sweat sooner (and sweat more). On top of that, I hide all of this when I leave my house, and never let on that I might be uncomfortable. Thank goodness for air conditioning. It's the one time I look forward to working in an office, even one that's two floors underground.

Summer clothing is also lost to me. I don't know about you, but I just feel silly in summery clothes. Summery clothes equal feminine, and as I keep mentioning, I lose a sense of that as the weight goes on. Summery to me equals dresses, sleeveless things, shorts, mini things. Ugh.

I manage my way through Summer, instead of genuinely enjoying it. I find the most comfort in (Jersey) plain colors, simple lines so as not to overly draw attention to the excess. It's not ideal, but my reality is that I spend four hours a day on a train, in 35c heat, when the air conditioning isn't working, and the train is delayed. If I'm trussed up like a turkey in a sleeveless pencil dress, I say again, ugh.

Winter is exponentially better for me. I get to choose velvets and (fake) fur and wool and earmuffs and those big furry 'Russian' hats (which look absurd on me), and not have much of a care in the world.

Last Summer, not only did I have ridiculous heat to deal with (UK summers consist of two days above 35c and then rain and 12c for the rest of it), but I had menopause symptoms as well. For a good four months I felt like I'd been rolled up in cling-film and put on a treadmill, in a sauna.

Time

I take one minute / hour / day at a time.

I have over a hundred pounds to lose, so it follows to me that this is realistically going to look like the mother of all chunks of 'diet and exercise' – a mountain one can't possibly climb. So, if I literally have to take each minute and get through it without eating, I do it. This is where the preparation and tools kick in.

The only analogy I could use is that this reminds me of when I was a tearaway teenager and would sneak off to the pub a few miles away from my house and have to walk back in the dead of night. We lived in the arse-end of nowhere and I'd be terrified of the dark. All kinds of sounds going on (foxes, owls, and whatnot) – to this day I don't know how I ever did it (and certainly wouldn't advocate doing that at all these days).

But I'd start. I'd take off my four-inch-bow-at-the-heel-80's stilettos. I'd put one foot in front of the other, and literally march home, barefoot.

I'd be looking at my feet the whole way, whispering out loud 'left, left, left -right, left' – like in those American soldier movies. I literally took one step at a time. The last hundred yards was the hardest; I had to walk past a deserted old farm barn that was super creepy, so I'd hike up my eighties-style walk-from-the-knee pencil skirt and sprint my little heart out. Legs, padded shoulders, and hair akimbo. Anecdote aside, if I literally have to remind myself what I'm doing and why I'm doing it by the minute – then I do that.

Toning Tables

These were 'all the rage' in the late eighties/early nineties, and I still drive past a salon that has them today. The common perception is that you lie on a table, which does all the work for you, but actually this is not the case. When the table lifts your leg, for instance, you are supposed to resist. When the table moves your butt, you are supposed to clench, and so on.

I bought a course of toning tables in the early nineties. In all honesty, I don't remember any astounding results - any more than you'd get from doing it at home with a friend helping with the resistance (not the clenching).

Toning has come a long way since then, and I don't think laying on a five-grand machine that lifts your leg up is going to come anywhere close to 'proper' toning exercises, like Pilates.

Still, it's nice to lie there and fantasize about a machine doing all the arduous work for you, isn't it? That is, until you pay for the privilege. Seriously, get your hoe on and go pull up some weeds in the garden instead.

Train Seats

'Wow, he's so big, he should have bought two tickets.'

I honestly once heard a person say that. Okay, it was on Facebook (the home of vitriol) but really, isn't that the most awful thing you can think about a fat person when they are on a train?

Of course, things like that stick in my mind and I end up thinking it myself. I've been commuting to London for three years now, and I use the little single pull-down seats just inside the train doors. I don't even go into the carriages. Sometimes, if I leave work early and get some obscure, middle-of-the-day train which will have almost no people on it, I will take a seat.

Strangely enough, it might seem like I'm generalizing, but I've noticed that other fat people seem drawn to sit next to me in these instances. Like an obese herding instinct, she thinks I'll completely understand and that she won't have to try and fold herself in half so that her hot sweaty thigh isn't clamped onto mine for the entire journey.

Err, well, not really, missus. I'm not sure any of us like rubbing up to a stranger's hot sweaty thigh. Although, I'd make an exception for Gerard Butler.

Triggers

I've learned a lot about triggers. These have been events in my life that cause me to feel I need to eat something. You could argue that these aren't 'triggers' but learned behavior. Many of us might eat when we are sad, eat if we've had a difficult day, eat to celebrate.

Most weight loss 'classes' teach you all about triggers. The danger is, if you ignore these triggers, they stack up. I also think it's a possibility that the bigger we get, the less we need a trigger or reason to overeat. By then, it's a habit.

If I've have a 'bad' day with food, the trick is to learn what triggered it. There is always something. Once I've nailed it, I decide how I am going to handle it if it happens again.

Personally, I wash my hands and put on some expensive hand cream. Make a glass of iced water in a posh glass (and drink it). Do something that will break the thought pattern. I try it, practice it, and make it a habit.

Another thing that works for me (if I get home from work and am tempted to order a pizza delivery with sides and ice-cream), is that I call my Dad, and have him come over for a cuppa. I wouldn't dare eat that in front of him. I know it's warped, but by the time he leaves, it's too late to eat and, hey, I didn't order in 12, 500 calories. Win.

U is for

Uniform

Now, I have to mention that in the current day and age, there is much more available in terms of clothes, to those who are a size 24+.

However, I see many overweight women, including myself, stick to a certain wardrobe and look, and there's a reason for this.

I pass many overweight women on the streets of London, and it's almost like looking in a mirror; I believe I know exactly what other women like me are going through when they get dressed in the morning.

They are wearing 'the uniform.' Women who are very overweight end up with the same wardrobe, usually for the same reasons.

Starting from the bottom:

Comfortable, flat shoes, possibly black trainers that are made to look like 'work' shoes. I doubt socks, unless the elastic has been cut because halfway through the day these start to cut off the circulation (and forget knee-highs, they should call them roll-downs). Possibly heel supports in the shoes, due to heel pain. Possibly a support bandage around the ankles, because of ankle pain. Knickers will not be control pants; those pants are made for someone who's a size eight and having a 'fat day.' For anyone else, they roll down your belly halfway through the day and cut off circulation to the legs entirely.

Skirt?

Hmm, doubtful because of leg-chafing. Most probably black trousers in as decent a fabric (as can be found at that size) with an elasticated back.

The bra will probably be an old one that we've 'worked in' because, with everything else a large woman has to put up with, who needs razor-wire? Sometimes it might be a decent un-wired bra, but we can never get the size right, so it makes our boobs look like long sausages.

On Top:

Whatever it is, will cover our belly, bum, and upper arms, and will probably be a plain color. It probably won't be a shirt; we're long past gaping shirtfronts by this stage, and again, one less thing to worry about.

The color might be black or white. However, occasionally clothing stores who stock our sizes, might treat us to an on-trend color. The material will be stretchy, preferably jersey, and the sleeves will preferably be ¾ length to cover our bingo-wings.

I have to say that as I age, I'm getting a teeny bit more adventurous in this regard, not least because clothing stores have cottoned-on. There's much more on-trend stuff these days that I don't mind wearing, and that I don't feel stupid in.

Also, I think my attitude has changed with age, (and a lot of therapy) and most days I no longer give a shit what people think of how I look. Or at least, I'm working on that. Upstairs in my spare bedroom, I have a laundry bin filled with some neatly folded clothes. This bin represents who I was. It has all the cloths in it that I used to love wearing. Even some brand-new clothes I've never worn. I'm not sure it's a healthy way to think. Every time I take the lid off that bin, I feel my personality come rushing out to greet me,

'Hi! Did you make your target weight yet!?'

'Yippee! Okay, get that black-taffeta mini skirt on, baby!'

I put the lid back on. I don't go in there too often.

V is for

Visualization

In amongst all the buzz about meditation and wellness lately, this concept seems to have been lost a bit. We're talking about creative visualization here, and its application to healing physical or psychological 'wounds' improving mood, self-esteem, and emotional glitches.

Imagining 'things' sounds very new age, doesn't it? But hey, if this is just one more tool that I can add to my arsenal to help with overeating, sign me up.

I recently downloaded a meditation 'pack' and part of the meditation was to imagine a 'pin-prick' of bright light in the centre of your chest, then gradually imagine it spreading outwards to literally cover the planet.

This sounds ridiculous, but when I was feeling isolated or low, this somehow re-connected me with the planet as a real and individual human being.

The visualization could be anything. During one session, and I can't believe I'm saying this, I 'saw' my third eye open. It was a big, regal, ancient, glorious, female eye (right in the centre of my forehead, like 'they' say). I honestly felt this was my 'spirit.' It was glamorous, confident, and fierce all at once. It said, 'I'm still here, you know.' It took me aback a bit. When I finished that session, I had a massive smile on my face for the rest of that day. Huge.

Other visualizations that help me are to imagine a spotlight of sun shining down on me, imagining it warm and protective, like a shield.

We can really get creative with this. If you practice meditation regularly, try an un-guided ten-minutes. Imagine what you would like to treat. It could be anything, low mood, boredom, seasonal affective disorder, negative feelings about food, perhaps even headaches, or some other physical pain.

Even if it's something you do to be free from thinking about food for a minute, it's all going to help, isn't it?

Once in the meditative state, create your own visualization.

Of course, it means practice, practice, practice.

Visualization suggestions:

- Curled up asleep as if you were two again
- Closing or opening filing cabinets in your brain
- Picking up smooth stones out of a cold forest stream
- Talking to your younger/older/confident/happy self
- Standing in bright sunlight

W is for

Waxing

See Beauticians

Weightwatchers (Diet Review)

Pros: Easy to count (points value for everything, although, see Gimmicks), nothing banned (you just decide whether it's worth it).

Cons: Expensive (in my opinion). The weightwatchers app is terrible, and the barcode scanner is absolutely dismal. The food database is fiddly and not as extensive as others. It's quite difficult to cancel the membership and be incredibly careful with 'automatic' renewals.

Tips: Use MyFitnessPal – it's extraordinarily better. Getting started: My best buddy started out on this in 2015, and since I had been feeling really low after putting (back) on over a stone, I wanted to give it a try. She seemed really committed ('Enough is enough, I don't want to cheat this time'), and so I decided that I need to grow up and get on with it too.

I decided to do the 'online' plan, which would motivate me, in part, to be responsible for my own destiny. I signed up, £29.85 for three months and completed all the information. I downloaded the mobile app.

I watched a few videos and mooched around the recipes. I put my scales out in the bathroom. I stood on scales (an achievement in itself). My piddly scales go up to 20st, and so I was expecting them to burst springs all over the floor, but my starting weight was less than I thought. Encouraging!

***

Weekly shopping list:

Fruit and veggies are completely free (do not need to be counted), and so I stocked up on as much of this as I could fit in my fridge. Plus, since I'm a 'picker' it had to be stuff I could just grab (since every time I walk past my fridge, my head is in it). Also, I do not have a microwave. And so:

Fruit & Veg: Nectarines, Clementine, Bananas, Yellow plums, Peaches, White Grapes, Avocados, Blueberries, Raspberries, Strawberries. Edamame bean and pea salad (200g box) – (really into edamame beans), 2 x ready-made salad bowls (time and inclination to make my own: nil), Bag cabbage and leek (stir-fry)

Meat, Cheeses, Dairy: Wafer-thin turkey slices & (Various, chargrilled etc.) cooked chicken slices (I know this is more expensive than buying a chicken and roasting it myself; however, I am super-picky with chicken, it HAS to be super-lean – I've been bordering on giving up meat altogether for a couple of years. 2 x Devonshire style yoghurts (Full-on-full-fat – since I don't buy yoghurt much at all I thought I'd buy 'the best'). Skimmed milk (I have this delivered by local milkman), 2 x bags (12) Mini 'light' cheeses (love these for grabby snacks, 1 point each). Butter (the full-on version).

Cereals and Breads: Breakfast cereal (not big on breakfast but good for evening snack), New York sesame bagels and small deli-wraps.

Sauces, Dressings etc.: Lime, ginger, and chili salad dressing, stir-fry sauce, 2 x unusual chutneys, low-fat custard. Cupboard: Snack-a-Jacks Cheese (the large round rice-cakes), Marmite, Water x 6 litre bottles (I drink gallons, thankfully -NO problems with water consumption), Lemon and Lime Jelly Pots, Sugar-Free (no room, time, or inclination to make my own), Salted Caramel Green Tea (smells amazing, tastes...well, like tea), extra strength aloe-vera juice with Manuka honey. Baked mini cheddars.

Most expensive on that list per category: Cooked meats £8. 35, Aloe-Vera juice £7. 85

Weekly cost: Based on shopping list provided, approximate: £60. 00 (again, it wouldn't be this every week because a lot of the stuff carries over).

* * *

I appreciate that some of my food choices might appear plain wrong to others

– a lot of the food is ready-prepared or ready cooked. If you look up 'Counting Calories with a Ballerina' on YouTube, I'd be interested to know whether this made you think differently about pre-prepared foods. I went straight into this. I had a couple of days off work I think, and so all I did all day was count and record, count, and record.

I lost almost forty pounds. I was almost a week away from being the lowest weight I'd been in eight or nine years. I cried once because I bought some clothes online, and they fit me. I did a double take in a full-length mirror once because I didn't recognise my outline. I actually stared myself up-and-down and thought Yeah, lady! You're doing it! For some inexplicable reason I still fell off that wagon (there have been many wagons). I decided to have Christmas 'off' and I regret that immensely. It was always 'I'll start back at it tomorrow' and that just kept going.

When I started this, I honestly felt like this was it in an 'epiphany' kind of way. I regret allowing myself to have time 'off' from it.

Which brings me nicely to...

Why

Over the years I've always interpreted the word diet as some 'thing' we put ourselves through. As you can see from the previous chapter, because of this, it was a 'thing' I could depart from.

A diet is something you 'start' and therefore, this insinuates to me, that a 'diet' has a fixed period of time. Therefore, it also has an 'end.'

I'm on a diet has come to mean that you are temporarily changing our eating habits in order to reach a (weight) goal. In my opinion, what we should actually be doing, is working on the psychological reasons for overeating -associated habits, and in particular, our dietary habits (see Habits).

A therapist once suggested to me that I am petulant when it comes to food. Meaning, I'm having that because I can, so I'm going to. (Imagine a three-year-old saying that: Yep, that's me).

My 'child' psyche is much more dominant that the 'parent' when it comes to food.

My 'parent' psyche is a self-whipping bitch, who pops up usually after I've eaten something and beats me up about it.

What I need to do is change the parent to a nurturer and swap the roles around: Have the parent encourage me to eat something nice before I've eaten it, and for the child to appreciate that I've eaten it.

Wow, I sound like such a frickin' hippy. I'm really not. But I appreciate that everything starts in the head. And, well, if you're wired wrong, you have to make some sense of it. This is my way of doing that.

In my preparation section, there's a task to think about this. I think it's definitely worth remembering the situations where I've overeaten and try and remember what I was thinking -before and after -to interpret that and change it. The 'changing it' part is where mindfulness and habits play in.

See? It's all connected. It doesn't matter how you choose to lose weight; I think we have to give ourselves the best chance we possibly can. And that includes studying every part of our being when it comes to over-eating.

X is for

X-Rated (Love, Sex, and Dating)

Their eyes meet across the room...

This tends to be the part I struggle with the most, being so overweight. I can clap eyes on someone (assuming I got out the door in the first place) *(see Bath Time)*, but then the return look tends to be the,

'Oh my god, fat bird, un-see, un-see!'

Which is fine. If I'm honest, what my eyes see is not what my heart wants, at all.

I find the whole 'meeting' someone to be incredibly contrived. These days, I'd rather eat glass, than 'meet' someone in a nightclub (which seems to be the only place for that kind of thing here in the UK). That's not really the basis for a stable, true, and honest relationship is it? I never saw anyone past the night before.

That's not to say I haven't met someone in a nightclub and taken them home (stop giggling, Jules), in fact, I would do it (and them) all over again. It was good clean safe fun, and I encourage anyone to get on that. As long as you can be safe. All us girls knew exactly where the other was at any given time -we had each other's backs there, and we always went home together.

I'm trying to recall a time when I was conscious about being fat while I went through my 'casual' nightclub sex phase. Granted, the drinks helped, but no, I was never bothered. I wasn't 'too overweight' back in my twenties.

I was wild, though, sheesh.

What I do remember, though, is that I was 'the fat friend' in one or two of those circumstances. I'd be the one holding the bags or guarding the drinks. But I got more than my fair share of spectacular shags.

One of the best was a guy that made me laugh like no other, and I find that spectacularly sexy. He wasn't a 'looker' at all, (think Roger De Courcey), but he just had me laughing 'til I cried or couldn't breathe every time I met him. Well, I was a goner. He made me weak at the knees.

I always wonder, once I've met someone, whether their kiss is going to ruin it for me. If you can't kiss right, I can't. I won't. But this guy was a phenomenal kisser. Holy cow, I felt it in my toes. Phew! Any self-image issues, gone.

What followed with 'Roger De Courcey' was the most surprising and memorable evening, night, morning, and afternoon, ever. It was electric (God, I'm laughing while I type this). This guy literally ripped my knickers off. Honestly. I've still got them somewhere. He tore them off. It was legendary, and I'll never forget it. Toe-curling, for sure. In those days, if you went home knicker-less with chin-burn (from kissing a man's face so hard for so long), you know you had an epic night.

Anyway, he was engaged. So, I gave him chlamydia as a wedding gift (that was everywhere, in the nineties). Just kidding, although he did blame me for it, I remember. I was checked and clean. He apologized to me for announcing, 'You gave me Chlamydia!' in my local pub. If the music hadn't been so loud, I'd never have gone back there. I wanted to accept his apology, but I just shook my head and walked away. The next day he was married, and that was the end of that.

* * *

After that was Brian, who had the most exotic tattoos, deepest brown eyes, and had a fat arse fetish. He was great fun. And my arse was fat. But he was a drunk. And married. And about to be shipped off to Iraq, or wherever they were deployed in those days.

* * *

In later years, as my self-esteem started to get in the way, I had a couple of 'internet relationships.' I wasn't really catfishing anyone, I was still physically social at that point. But one guy met me in a chat room and sent me poems every day for six months.

Jude, his name was. Told me he was a stock market trader in New York who was into ice hockey and good wine. I liked the whole mystery about it, and I was free to imagine that he looked like the guy in the painting 'Like a Boss' by Gabe Leonard. I'm sure he had a pre-conceived fantasy about me too (well, I know he did). Seventeen years on, I still have that sense of mystery when it comes to Jude, even though we haven't emailed for four years or more. I have a very secret fantasy about meeting him. Entirely mapped out down to the shoes and lighting.

So, I never want to meet him. I want to keep 'that.' Reality is not where Jude and I belong. He's married anyway. And I'm fat. I kept all our conversations, and I do read them occasionally; although, they have an unfortunate cringe-factor now. We were role-playing, after all.

* * *

The early 2000's was when I really retreated into myself. I'd changed careers from being a sales rep, which I was amazing at, to an I. T Analyst.

All of a sudden, I was in a world surrounded by I. T. geeks, who had questionable social skills. Unless you were fluent in Unix, there was no hope. Most of them had grown up in their mother's garage, programming on their Spectrums, or whatever it was in those days.

Some of them would look at the floor if you came within three feet of them. Since they clearly hadn't really had to deal with the whole female thing, they turned to their obnoxious selves, fat females even less.

I received a variety of negative reactions, which probably contributed to my ever-decreasing self-esteem.

The most common was talking over me, as if I were invisible. On one occasion, I encountered a man who had adamantly decided that, as I was fat and working in I. T, that I must be gay. And he said it often, in front of my colleagues. Homosexuality is a complete non-issue as far as I am concerned. Human beings deserve to love whomever they love. Life's too short for that shit. I am heterosexual. It's all just so absurd to me I don't even know why that warrants a mention -only that my I. T. colleague's remarks hurt me more than I'd care to admit. To the point that I had second thoughts about changing careers right about then.

* * *

I digress. While going through this, I dabbled with (three) casual encounters with people I'd met online -far, far more dangerous than meeting someone in a nightclub. Again, I don't really remember feeling self-conscious about my weight (more conscious about not being murdered). To them I think, it was just something to shag; I could have been a sheep for all they cared. How I didn't have my throat slit during that time, I have no clue. Particularly after a 'dirty' weekend with a rich guy who was older than my Dad. The whole situation was sad, ugly, and not one that lifts the spirit by any stretch of the imagination. So, you know, I stopped doing that, while I still had a tiny shred of self-respect left.

By then I think I was well into the 'dark zone' in terms of self-esteem. Weight was piling on because, financially, I was pretty loaded, earning between £200 and £500 a day with the I. T jobs. I wasn't wealthy, but I certainly had more money than I knew what to do with. So, eating out or ordering in was not a financial concern.

I was also living in hotels from Monday through Friday, and so the hotels fed me. And fed me well. The cost was deductible, so even less concern about what I was ordering.

* * *

In 2003, I met someone online, and we had an intense video relationship. He was Mike, from Pensacola in Florida, and we spoke for hours every single day.

He was six feet two, all-American, lean, healthy, beautiful-looking, perfect teeth, funny, intelligent, and spoke his mind and feelings. He could have been in movies.

Even working away, I could log on and get on video chat with him. I think I was definitely catfishing him by then; although, I told him every day that I was fat, he just used to say,

'You're not fat.' (Fat women are very clever when it comes to webcams).

He was just so beautiful that I fought him all the way. I resisted getting into a virtual relationship with him, but he absolutely chased me down and insisted that we could make it work. He was adamant and relentless. A couple of months in, on video chat, he looked right at the cam and told me,

'I love you.' (And it choked him up, it really did; it was an epiphany for him, too).

I didn't say it back. I was fat and I was conning him, and I'd say so.

Still, he insisted and persevered. Eventually, I caved.

I felt loved, you see. And I think being fat with low self-esteem I was vulnerable for a moment. He'd say, 'Okay, okay, you're 'fat'' (as if humoring me), 'but let's just pretend-like...'

He was giving me permission to pretend. He still didn't believe I was fat, and I kept insisting I was. And he kept thinking I was joking. Over the years my negative self-doubts in this respect started to make him a little bit pissed off. He said it felt like I was making light of his feelings, as if I didn't believe him.

This sounds absurd, but I was in a relationship with Mike for eight years. He WAS in my life and there was no one else, that whole time. (Well, once, early on, I shagged a stranger in a hotel and almost dislocated my hip, but it was just that once).

When I walked in my front door, he was (virtually) there waiting for me. I'd chat to him while doing my housework, we'd talk about our day, and we'd make plans. I mean, real plans. We'd laugh together, we'd cry together, we did everything together, we'd argue, fight, make up. We bought each other gifts, and we'd send each other money; we'd help each other when we needed it. I still believe, it was an honest-to-god relationship. Virtually.

I was so in love with this guy, I couldn't imagine him not being in my life. Subconsciously, though, I felt I was 'in deeper' than I'd be able to explain if I ever met him for real. That made me panic, and so my self-esteem was secretly evaporating, for all those years.

My faith in him was such that we both wanted a physical relationship. We were talking marriage and everything. So, we both 'bit the bullet' and decided to get together for real, seven years after we'd met online.

In the run up to that, I'd had surgery to have a Gastric Band. Make of that what you will – you'd probably be right. Right around that time, I'd found his profile on a dating website. Horrified (absurdly). We fought; he said he needed a physical 'relationship' and so we decided to push onwards: On the 20th of October 2010 I flew out to Pensacola. I was terrified but resigned. We both agreed that this whole situation was absurd, and we needed to get on with 'it.' There was a nagging feeling against the pessimist in me, that it could really work and that I'd been panicking for no reason all these years, because I was fat.

So, we both decided out loud,

'Eff-it -whatever happens, happens.'

I swear, right up until I got on that plane, I was telling him, 'I'm fat.' Truly.

After eight or so hours I got off the plane and collected my bags. On the way out, I went into the bathroom.

No turning back now.

I freshened up. Took off my travel socks, re-applied deodorant, mascara, and lip gloss. Stopped hyperventilating.

Mike had already texted me, saying he was in a bar having a coke and burst into tears that he was so happy I was here finally. He was telling complete strangers in the bar about it. I stood in the bathroom and considered the last seven years. I was about to find out if those two thousand, five hundred and fifty-five days had been real, or whether I'd wasted them. This could make or break me, literally.

One more 'Eff-it' and a last look in the mirror and I turned to leave. My stomach was doing triple-back-flips.

I'm not that fat, come on now -you've lost a load lately; it'll be fine.'

I remember turning a corner and there he was with a gift and a bunch of roses in hand, crying like a baby.

Then I burst into great wailing sobs, and we just held on to each other for a good five minutes. We just stood there and cried. We couldn't let go of each other. Then we kissed and cried some more.

All the strangers around us were staring and saying, 'Aww, that's so sweet' while walking by, or 'Way to go!.' I felt like I was in a movie. This made us both cry even more, until it was just funny.

As I'd been awake for twenty-two hours, I was delirious. I felt like I was floating in a dream. When we checked in at the hotel I'd booked, Mike said to the receptionist, 'I'd like a key please, I'm her boyfriend.'

Mike never once gave off the vibe that he was even remotely disappointed. He absolutely wasn't, it was real.

I immediately relaxed and was almost sad that I'd worried about it for seven years.

We explored the hotel and beach a bit, and I opened his completely unexpected gift: a first-edition kindle. He knew me, through and through.

That night, I showered, put pajamas on and passed out. Mike slept on the floor out of respect. I thought it was sweet. I was so tired I don't even remember going to sleep.

The entire trip was like floating in a daydream; it was perfect. We drove to New Orleans the next day and spent the night there, in my favorite place (I'd visited several times). I had booked a suite in the Ritz Carlton -because why not.

I took him to all my favorite haunts and taught him how to make proper tea. Proper British style, not that American crap. Blasphemy.

You might wonder by now, what the sex was like... Thinking back, it was loving, and you know, he was very well equipped, with energy to match -he was a bit younger than me, after all. But I don't remember there being any soul-wrenching tenderness really. In fact, sitting here now, it's uncomfortable to think about. I think me being fat did hold me back a bit, and prevented me from doing certain things, in certain places. Although, I flat out laughed in his face when he asked me to take a shower with him.

'Mike' I said, 'I'm five feet tall, don't be ridiculous.' He laughed. 'So? It'll be fun.'

Oh, the imagery. I did love that about him, though. He was 'game.'

On the last morning, we shagged for like three hours –I about passed out. When it came to leaving Mike and flying home, it was traumatic. We couldn't let go of each other, and I about cried all the way home. I'd have stayed if it hadn't made me illegal.

'I'm crying so hard right now' he texted me, 'You wore me out this morning' I replied. 'Wanted to send you home right 12' he said.

So, over the following months, we resumed our online thing. I think we were both getting increasingly frustrated with the situation. Whereas we'd made enthusiastic plans before, the plans I pushed for were definitely met with hesitance.

I made another trip out in April the following year: 2011. I rented an apartment that time. I remember the first night we walked into the apartment, I sat down, and he shifted up next to me. I burst into tears.

'I hope those are tears of happiness' he said.

They were. But what I didn't tell him was that they were also tears of hopelessness. Something in me knew that this was likely how things were going to stay. It just wasn't going to work. I'd been right, after all, in all these years.

So, I was there for a week. We went grocery shopping together and all things related to 'playing house' together. He went to work in the day. Pretending, again. It was great, again. But still, it wasn't 'going' anywhere.

And I left again.

Our relationship definitely cooled after that. Not for want of trying. But in actual fact, being fat wasn't an issue at all. It was him. He was hesitant about following through, on decisions I wanted us to make, like who was going to live where and so on. The fat was absolutely never a 'thing.'

Surprisingly, it was me that ended the relationship. On Christmas Day, 2011, no less. He hadn't called or texted or video-called that entire day. So, everything that had been bubbling up in my mind made me roar.

We finally video-chatted, and I ended the relationship. I realised that I didn't even like him anymore, and I said so. We were both crying. Who'd have thought, a fat girl rejecting a man. But reject him I did.

I needed to hear him say, out loud, 'Goodbye Samantha.' And, as per my request, he did.

Then I clicked off the video call, deleted the history, un-installed the app, and un-plugged. Epic mic-drop on my part.

* * *

I was quite proud that I'd done it, and I was convinced that we'd have been going around in those same circles for another eight years if I hadn't acted.

Within a month, he'd gone back to God (his parents were fervently religious -I am NOT -and they refused to acknowledge me as anything other than a harlot who had pulled their son away from God). He got back together with his high school sweetheart even, married her in a Japanese garden (which is what we had planned), bought her kids a puppy (which is what we had planned), and taught her kids how to play video games (something we did together).

I was exhausted, drained, felt like I'd had eight years stolen from me -and had no inclination whatsoever about meeting anyone. Just wasn't interested. In any kind of relationship with a man: virtual or not. Fat or no. That's it. I'm done. Finito. The End.

* * *

Here we are in the present then. Just about. My darling bestie convinced me a couple of years ago to 'get out there' again. I think everyone around me is 'worried' about me becoming a dying spinster surrounded by cats. All except me, actually.

So, I relented. I put a profile up on POF.com and had the following dates:

- Heavy-set bearded hippie with a crocheted man-bag and an ancient tee-

shirt he'd obviously scraped up off the floor that morning. No.
- Photographer who was repulsed by me and stared at his phone the whole meet, before making his excuses and running away.
- Bloke who still lived with his mum and looked like a short Mr. Bean with glasses. He said no to me because I was 'too successful.' *Wait, what?* Screw you, buddy –I'm not apologizing for that (or moving in with your sodding mother).
- Bloke who had three dates with me, we got on great, he was funny, easy to be around, didn't seem to mind the fatness and, you know, shaggable. Never called me after that. (His wife obviously returned from being out of town for a few days).
- Bloke who (never got a date from me, but) had a shirtless profile (ugh), and opened the conversation 'Hey, babe.' (Ugh). On closer inspection, I realised he was a fellow commuter on my train in the morning. He was constantly whistling tunes (which makes me want to commit murder) and had a weird-shaped head. No.

End of that phase, for sure.

* * *

I'd always thought that these dating websites are way worse than nightclubs, most of the men on it were looking for a supermodel, despite all being 'not all that' themselves. I know what you're thinking, you're absolutely right, it's that old saying isn't it: A real person should love you for who you are, not what you look like.

Really? Honestly? That saying is like nails down a chalkboard for me. To prove this saying entirely wrong, I did a little experiment. I joined a dating site (The Telegraph one if you're interested).

I wrote a bright intelligent witty profile and I put a full-length picture of myself right up there, overweight, roly-poly (although very well turned-out, I have to say). For each week I ticked a variety of boxes and changed my photograph. Here are the results:

Ticked 'Full-figured' Photo: Full-length –No profile views. No messages.

Ticked 'A few extra pounds' Photo: Full-Length –A few views, one message. Asking me to buy him a profile. Sod off.

Ticked 'A few extra pounds' Photo: Face only –Several views, no messages.

Ticked 'Curvy' Photo: Face only –Forty-two views, four messages.

* * *

This puts me in mind of a quote from a movie I once heard:

> *'Don't you think a woman has more to offer than the way she is dressed?'*
> *'Of course, but men are such visual creatures, darling, so it's a good place to start.'*
> – *'W.E' directed by the incomparable Madonna Ciccone.*

I'm fat, I'm single, and I'm not spending another single ounce of energy to find a man who is just going to take up space in a life that has no room for him.

I'm also probably never shagging again either. I'm completely fine with that. I could write a book about my sexual escapades. Been there, seen it, done it, got the medal for it.

In any case, menopause has changed me to the point that if Gerard Butler showed up at my door, naked and in the rain, I'd slam the door in his face.

Okay, maybe I'd get a towel.

.

Y is for

Yoga

See Exercise

Z is for

Zee End of the Book

Oh, come on, really? I couldn't find a Z-word. Not one that I have extraordinarily strong feelings about anyway. This, though, is a good opportunity for me to have a final reflection.

One would think that, since the Author (ahem, me, thank you very much) knows so much about weight loss, that she'd be a perfect weight by now.

Well, no. I'm still very overweight. I know everything in this book because I've done it. The point is I've done it many times over, and I know what works.

I just haven't *kept* doing it, and it's that which I am working on. Just like everyone else. I'm learning coping skills, I'm learning to be kind to myself, and perhaps, most of all, I'm learning that, while I figure this out, no-one on this planet has any right or basis to judge my appearance (something which bothers me, immensely).

A cognitive behavioral therapist once told me that I'd taught myself to fail. That in my head, failing (at weight loss), is something I have to do. That it's just a normal thing, according to my mind.

My most successful weight loss of recent years was using Weight Watchers (at home, not going to class, see Plateaus). As I mentioned, I lost over forty pounds, cried with happiness because clothes actually fit me, and for the first time in several years, I was about to be the lowest weight I'd been in that time.

But I still failed. I got complacent and petulant decided to view Christmas as a 'vacation.' And then I never ended the vacation.

So, I've gone back to basics. I've decided I have to change my attitude about myself, and then my attitude about food, before I can expect to change anything else. I really hope you can join me.

Bibliography

'20/20' Investigates Diet Pill Ads'
Retrieved April 2021, from ABC News:
http://bit.ly/mbff-bib1

'Chris Mapletoft parents 'shocked' over diet pills death.'
BBC News. Retrieved April 2021 from:
http://bit.ly/mbff-bib2

'Imported Fenproporex-based Diet Pills from Brazil: A Report of Two Cases.'
Cohen, P. A. (2009, 24(3), 430-433 Journal of General Internal Medicine. Retrieved April 2021 from:
http://bit.ly/mbff-bib3

'Appetite Suppressants and Valvular Heart Disease.'
Devereux, R. B. (1998). The New England Journal of Medicine, 339(11), 765-767. Retrieved April 2021 from:
http://bit.ly/mbff-bib4

'Diet Pills and Heart Disease.'
Krumholz, H. (1997). Retrieved April 2021 from:
http://bit.ly/mbff-bib5

'Cardiac arrest in the setting of diet pill consumption.'
Makaryus, J.N., & Makaryus, A. N. (2008). American Journal of Emergency Medicine, 26(6). Retrieved April 2021 from:

http://bit.ly/mbff-bib6

'Diet pill usage in patients with bulimia nervosa.'
Mitchell, J. E., Pyle, R. L., & Eckert, E. D. (1991). International Journal of Eating Disorders, 10(2), 233-237. Retrieved April 2021 from:
http://bit.ly/mbff-bib7

'Features associated with diet pill use in individuals with eating disorders.'
Reba-Harrelson, L., Holle, A.V., Thornton, L. M., Klump, K. L., Berrettini, W. H., Brandt, H.,Bulik, C. M. (2008). Eating Behaviors, 9(1), 73-81. Retrieved April 2021 from:
http://bit.ly/mbff-bib8

Epigraph

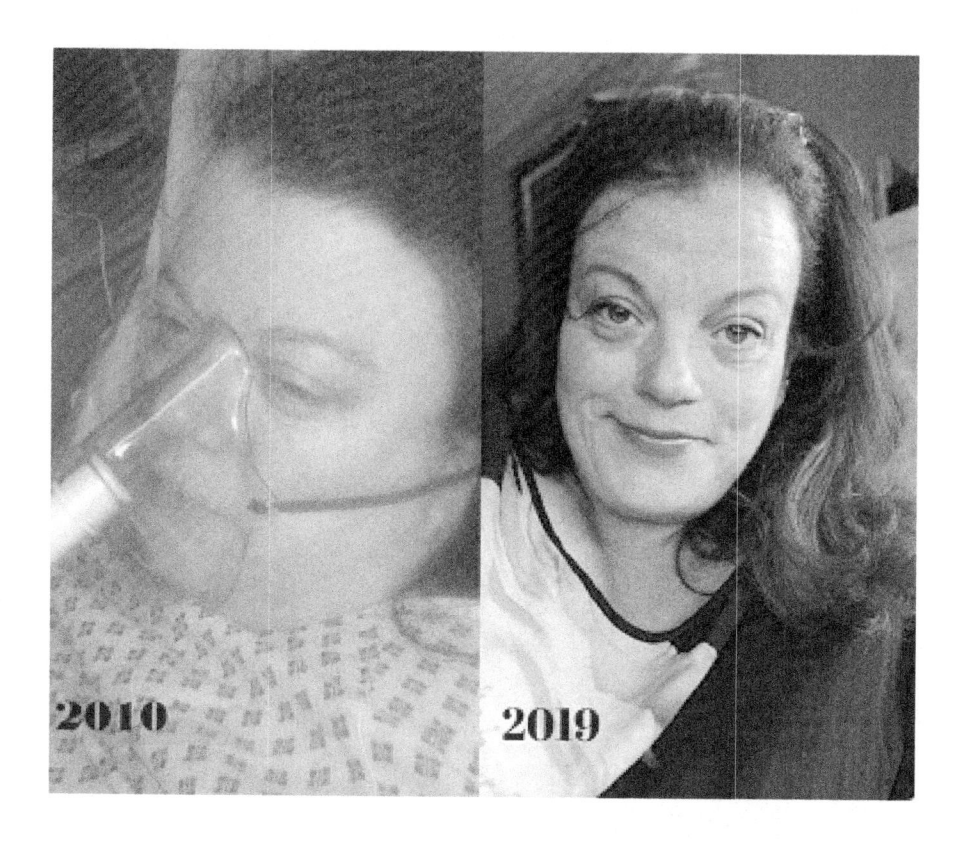

2010 **2019**

Since writing this book, Samantha has spent several hundred hours researching the way her brain behaved the way it did, in order to heal from decades of dieting and self-mutilation and live a life free from self-consciousness and low self esteem. She has been awarded qualifications in:

- Master Mindfulness Practitioner
- Cognitive Behavioural Therapy
- Skilled Helping and Talk Therapy
- Neuro Linguistic Therapy
- Counselling and Hypnotherapy
- Anxiety & Depression Therapy

She has lost fifty pounds so far, by NOT dieting.

The sequel to 'My Big Fat Fat' is in progress.

She runs a little tech company, teaches at Udemy, maintains a blog at samanthadee.com and is having a blast writing her first fiction series in the Urban Fantasy genre.

She is currently selling her house and entire life, to go live by the sea and write books.

More by Samantha

Journals & Workbooks:

- The Thirty Day Wellness Journal. https://bit.ly/3DW-workbook
- Plan Your Life: Dream it, Plan it, Do it. https://bit.ly/PYL-workbook
- Find Your Passion. https://bit.ly/FYP-workbook
- A New Dawn. https://bit.ly/AND-workbook

Online Courses:

- Plan Your Life: Dream it, Plan it, Do it. http://bit.ly/yesplanmylife
- Find Your Passion. http://bit.ly/discovermypassion
- A New Dawn. http://bit.ly/newdawnsammy

Blog:

- My Big Fat Blog. http://bit.ly/mybigfatblog
- Quitting the Rat Race (A visualization concept). http://bit.ly/myfakejournal

Fiction:

- 'Wings on the Loose' The Dragon Hatcher Diaries, Book One. https://bit.ly/lovesammydee

An Excerpt from 'The Sequel'

Transitioning is getting prepared for a coming change. As I said in my previous book, if you don't prepare, you fail. It's that simple.

When summer is coming, you put away your winter coats and gloves, and get out tee-shirts and bikinis. When winter is coming you get Tyrion Lannister on your side (unless he's dead already, is he? I should catch up).

It's also important to remember that in order to change you have to actually do something different.

I was chatting to a friend recently, and she was telling me about all the fruit, veg, and healthy whatnots she buys and then ends up throwing away.

It's all very well to buy this stuff (and it looks great in your cupboards and all) but you have to consume it too.

It's about two things, preparation and FEAR. It's no use buying a load of salad items if it's snowing outside and you're aching for a big bowl of chilli.

Fear has come from the Diet and Food Industry. With the exception of very few (even Jamie Oliver scares me), we are shown that oats rolled on the thighs of vestal virgins from the outer Mongolian floating mountains should be readily available in our cupboards. And if it isn't, we tend to say, 'bugger it' and make a bowl of cereal and watch Strictly on telly. Who needs that crap, right?

***

Mailing list for release announcements: https://bit.ly/SubToSammyDee

Or follow Sammy Dee's Amazon Author page at https://bit.ly/followsammy

About the Author

Writing under various guises, Samantha has been penning stories, editing anthologies, and writing non-fiction since she could hold a pen. In primary school at age seven, she filled up an entire writing book with a story about a haunted house.

In secondary school, her English teacher said, 'If she quits clowning around, she'll be great at this.' (before being suspended for 'clowning around.') Her fiction debut, 'The Dragon Hatcher' – an Urban Fantasy – is to be released in 2021.

Email Samantha at nittygrittysam@gmail.com or follow her on most social media.

You can connect with me on:

- https://samanthadee.com
- http://bit.ly/tw-sammydee
- https://bit.ly/lovesammydee
- http://bit.ly/ig-sammydee
- http://bit.ly/gr-sammydee

Subscribe to my newsletter:

- http://bit.ly/sub-sammydee

Also by Samantha Dee

Samantha is a multi-genre independent Author. She writes non-fiction as Samantha Dee, fiction as S. Marie Diegutis and has edited an Anthology of horror fiction as Samantha Diegutis.

The Thirty Day Wellness Journal
A lovely, high-quality, full-color wellness journal to record sleep, nutrition, positivity, gratitude and feelings with space for personal expression.
   https://bit.ly/bm-30daywellness

Plan Your Life: Dream it, Plan it, Do it.
A workbook which enables radical life change by examining your current situation, refining your ideals and then shaping those into an actionable roadmap to a life re-built.
   https://bit.ly/bm-planyourlife

Find Your Passion Workbook
Fifty guided questions to help you re-energize and re-ignite your life's passions!
   https://bit.ly/bm-findyourpassion

A New Dawn Workbook

Thirty days of wellness to discover new practices and re-kindle old ones.

https://bit.ly/bm-anewdawn